MANCHEST
FOOTBAL

#CHAMPIONS 2011/2012

06. **THE DAY WE MADE HISTORY**
May 13, 2012

18. **IN THE HEROES' WORDS**
What They Said

30. **MANCINI**
The Miracle Man

36. **SIX OF THE BEST**
The Key Games

54. **STORY OF THE SEASON**
Step by Step to Glory

72. **TITLES GONE BY**
1937 and 1968 . . .

76. **2011-2012**
Complete Statistics

78. **TOGETHER WE ARE CHAMPIONS**

Content: David Clayton. **Match reports:** Neil Jeffries. **Statistics compiled by** Trevor Hartley. **Photos:** MCFC offical photographer Sharon Latham, PA Pics.
Produced by Trinity Mirror Sport Media. **Executive Editor:** Ken Rogers. **Senior Editor:** Steve Hanrahan. **Senior Art Editor:** Rick Cooke. **Editor:** Paul Dove.
Writers: Alan Jewell, Gary Gilliland. **Production:** James Cleary, Roy Gilfoyle, William Hughes. **Design:** Colin Sumpter, Glen Hind, Lisa Critchley

THE DAY HISTORY WAS MADE

If you have waited 44 years for a title, perhaps the only way to win it is in sensational, spine tingling fashion with the fans on the edge of their seats and the whole nation tuned in to the greatest finale in the history of the Barclays Premier League.

The sun, albeit a fading one, was still shining over the Etihad Stadium as Sergio Aguero drew back his blue right boot with just 100 seconds of a truly remarkable season remaining on the clock. Suddenly, a massive blue moon was now shining brighter than the sun by the time Sergio's flashing shot hit the back of the Queens Park Rangers net.

The scoreboard, showing City 2-1 down just four minutes earlier, flashed up its Champion message.

MANCHESTER CITY 3
QUEENS PARK RANGERS 2
Etihad Stadium, 13.05.12

Had it really happened? Was it really over? Was Roberto Mancini's victory run on the touchline, pursued by his elated coaching staff, the signal that the City faithful could finally wake up to an exciting new dawn with the Premier League trophy wrested from their greatest rivals? Yes, headline writers at newspapers all over the country were preparing to make it official . . .

CITY DREAMS COME TRUE . . . CRAZY, BLUE AND THE BEST . . . CITY SUPREME AFTER MIRACLE AT THE ETIHAD . . . MANCINI'S CRAZY GANG MAKE EVERY LAST SECOND COUNT . . .

This was the game that dreams are made of. This was the day the legend of Lee, Bell, Book and the rest, watching and beaming from the stands, was finally overtaken by the spirit of Zabaleta, Dzeko, and Aguero - the goalscorers who helped make history.

And let's complete that roll of honour because this was a team display in every way . . . Hart, Lescott, Kompany, Clichy, Silva, Y. Toure, De Jong, Barry, Nasri, Tevez, Balotelli . . . these are the other heroes who competed in this game of games and can forever say: 'I was there and part of one of the most eventful days in City's history'. And not forgetting Messrs Pantilimon, Richards, Kolarov and Milner, restricted to the bench but as one with their teammates every precious second of the way.

Even the QPR players were elated, not for City's remarkable moment of glory, but for the fact that they had survived at the other end of the Premier League on a day when so many ups and downs were settled.

Rangers lost, but perhaps earned their lifeline on a day when nothing could be taken for granted from the moment referee Mike Dean signalled the start of what

>>

turned out to be 95 minutes of football that proved to be gut wrenching and nerve-shredding in parts for fans and players, but ultimately inspirational and sensational.

Another newspaper headline summed all of this up perfectly in assessing what City had gone through: THEY ALL AGED 44 YEARS IN JUST 93 MINUTES!

This made reference, of course, to our last Championship win in 1968, but this is 2012 and it will not be the year but the date - Sunday, May 13 - that will never be forgotten as the definitive example of why the Barclays Premier League is hailed the world over as the greatest football show on earth.

Not since 1989 had the finale to a title race been quite so dramatic. Edin Dzeko instigated his rescue mission when it seemed all might be lost with QPR 2-1 ahead and the clock showing that two of the five minutes of stoppage time had elapsed. The tall striker rose above his marker

THE STORY OF A REMARKABLE DAY AS IT UNFOLDED ON MCFC TWITTER...

Teams being read out for the final time this season. Warm cheers for the three former MCFC players in the QPR ranks today.

And here come the teams! The Etihad erupts to welcome their sky blue heroes. Ticker tape flies down from the South Stand. HERE WE GO!

Glorious atmosphere in the Etihad on this, one of the biggest days in our beloved club's history. Teams in the tunnel. CUME ON CITY!

Blue Moon rings out and the game gets under way! COME ON CITY!!

2. Incredible noise punctuates the opening stages. City seeing most of the ball, looking to get in their stride early doors.

3. Tevez tries to battle through and City have an early corner.

5. Great determination from Aguero who chases a lost cause and sets up Tevez for a shot. The ball comes out to Yaya who blazes over.

9. City calling all the shots so far. QPR with everyone back soaking up this early pressure and looking to break when the opportunity arises.

10. Roberto will be pleased with his team's start. Nasri hits an effort from way out that doesn't trouble Paddy Kenny in the QPR goal.

12. QPR fans erupt as news filters through of a goal for Stoke against Bolton which would keep them up if the score stays the same.

15. Kenny needs two goes to save Silva's cross with Tevez lurking but then saves well from a driven effort by the Spaniard.

17. City need to up the tempo a bit. Couple of stray and nervy passes creeping in. Barton goes down after a challenge with Barry.

20. Patient build-up from City on the edge of the QPR box. Zabaleta fires in a cross which evades the flying Aguero.

22. Barry fouls Cisse and QPR have a free-kick 22 yards out and to the left of the City penalty area. Danger here.

24. Cisse fires in the setpiece through the wall but Hart is on hand to save.

25. SWP (Shaun Wright-Phillips) handles on the edge of his own box and City have a dangerous setpiece of their own now.

26. After a brief flurry from the Rs, City have regained the impetus here, pegging the visitors back, but still not really creating much.

31. Lovely work from Yaya who finds Tevez with his back to goal. The Argentine sets up Silva who drives his effort just wide. Much better!

35. Yaya looks like he's struggling, hopefully just with cramp. Aguero gets in behind but his cross eludes Tevez.

37. Tevez looks for a one-two with Nasri in the box but the French star's return ball is lacking and QPR clear away.

38. GOAL FOR CITY!!!!! Pablo Zabaleta!!!!

39. Kenny got a big hand to Zaba's effort but the ball looped into the corner. WOO HOO!!!

41. The Etihad shook to its foundations following that most crucial of goals. City immediately after another.

43. Yaya Toure's injury appears to be enough for him not to continue and Nigel De Jong is set to come on any minute.

44. And here is the change. A fabulous reception for the player whose heroics at Newcastle last week set up today's title decider.

45. All change at Stoke. Bolton are now leading meaning QPR need a result here. This might see them come out more and work in City's favour.

And that's half time! MCFC 1-0 QPR at the break thanks to Pablo Zabaleta.

Teams are back out! Second half coming right up. Gonna try and hold the emotions together for you all this half, dear MCFC Twitterers.

Continued on page 13

>> to meet a David Silva corner and bullet a header past the defiant Paddy Kenny to suddenly make everyone believe the miracle was possible. The Etihad exploded and those who were on the edge of their seats were now living every tackle and header as Nigel De Jong carried the ball forward, picking out Sergio Aguero 30 yards from goal.

Aguero passed to Mario Balotelli, and continued his run. Balotelli swivelled and and poked the ball back into Aguero's path. Taiwo tried to close the Argentinian down, but was beaten by the first touch and history beckoned.

Aguero smashed his shot past Kenny and the stadium erupted. The striker had brought joy and happiness to the blue side of Manchester as the celebrations begun.

The opening exchanges of this game now seemed light years away, but it is important to understand the ecstasy and the agony that had previously unfolded to truly gauge the impact of the overtime celebrations. City, trying to be patient and controlled on a day of high emotion, made the breakthrough every fan was hoping for six minutes before half time. Pablo Zabaleta had previously scored just six goals in a ten-year professional career, but now he was in seventh heaven. Goalkeeper Kenny got two hands to Zabaleta's shot, but the ball looped high into the air before finding the net.

Even when City lost the influential Yaya Toure to a hamstring injury, everyone was expecting them to build on their lead. However, Rangers scored with their first real attack after 48 minutes. Joleon Lescott failed to make a decisive headed clearance from a hopeful forward ball by Shaun Wright Phillips, allowing Djibril Cisse to capitalise and beat Joe Hart.

Rangers' elation was matched only by the despair of losing Joey Barton to a senseless red card after 54 minutes after he swung an elbow at Carlos Tevez, and then compounded his moment of madness by lunging at Aguero and putting his head in Kompany's face.

City now had the extra man advantage, but the game was turned upside down after 65 minutes when Armand Traore raced forward down the left and fired in a cross that produced a fine diving header from Jamie Mackie.

The tension as the game went into added time was swamping everyone, not least because of the news from Sunderland that arch-rivals Manchester United had secured a lone goal victory that, at this point, meant their name was once again on the Premier League trophy.

But City are a very different club these days, and a world class squad, backed by a world class attitude dictates that nothing is ever lost. It pointed us towards that spectacular finish as Dzeko and Aguero inspired unconfined joy across the Etihad.

It was simply unbelievable.

MANCHESTER CITY: Hart, Zabaleta, Lescott, Kompany, Clichy, Silva, Y Toure (De Jong 46 mins), Barry (Dzeko 69 mins), Nasri, Aguero, Tevez (Balotelli 76 mins). Subs not used: Pantilimon, Richards, Kolarov, Milner.

QPR: Kenny, Onuoha, Ferdinand, Hill, Taiwo, Mackie, Derry, Barton, Wright-Phillips, Zamora (Bothroyd 76 mins), Cisse (Traore 59 mins). Subs not used: Cerny, Gabbidon, Taarabt, Buzsaky, Campbell.

GOALS: Zabaleta 39, Dzeko 90, Aguero 90, Cisse 48, Mackie 66.

REFEREE: Mike Dean. **ATTENDANCE:** 48,000

Continued from page 9

City get the second half under way. Nine months of football boils down to the biggest 45 minutes of the club's history.

45. The Blues are out of the traps quickly and have a free kick after a foul on De Jong. Nasri attempts to catch Kenny out but it goes over.

47. Out of nowhere QPR have a goal. Confusion at the back and Cisse latches on and fires past Hart! 1-1.

50. It was Lescott's off-balance back header that let the Rs striker in. City can't let that effect them and need to hit right back!

51. City corner comes out to Zabaleta who fires right back in and Aguero almost steers it into the net from two yards out!

53. The linesman flags after an off the ball incident between Barton and Tevez. Looked like an elbow from the former City man.

54. And Barton gets a red card! And he clashes with Aguero on his way off. A mass brawl breaks out now!

55. Absolute chaos here, but the upshot is City have a free kick on the edge of the box and QPR have ten men!

57. Order restored... just! Tevez fires in the free-kick. Barry almost turns it in and City have a corner!

58. QPR sub Cisse for Traore and City have yet another corner.

59. Kenny saves on the line. The ball didn't go in despite the City claims. No time to catch your breath here.

61. QPR in full retreat mode but a draw is no good for them either. City putting in lots of crosses but lacking in some height up front.

66. QPR SCORE! Mackie with the final touch on the break away and City are behind!

67. Edin Dzeko set to come on to provide the height we're lacking up front.

70. City keep coming but keep hitting a red and white brick wall. Barry is off for Dzeko.

71. Kenny saves Tevez's header at the back post but it keeps on coming. City throwing everything at this now!

73. Tevez beats two but his shot slices well wide. Mario Balotelli about to come on.

74. Carlos Tevez comes off for Mario Balotelli, 15 minutes of the season to go. City need two goals from somewhere to win the league.

77. Kenny with a fine save to deny Dzeko. City's latest corner is fired away but they keep coming.

80. Ten minutes to go. City fans praying for something to break for the Blues. Please don't let it be our hearts!

85. Still nothing going for City and it's getting harder and harder to watch. QPR playing on the edge of their own box clearing everything.

89. Mario with a shot but for what feels like the hundredth time today it's blocked. Another corner coming up.

91. GOAL FOR CITY! DZEKO!!! COME ON LADS!!!!

95. AGUERO SCORES AND WINS THE LEAGUE!!!!

City fans on the pitch! The league is ours!!! Final score City 3-2 QPR. UNBELIEVABLE!!!

VINCENT KOMPANY:

'We knew Manchester United were winning but we always said we had to focus on our game. We knew we had to win. We never stopped believing. Life is too short to throw away such a chance. We nearly did but we deserve to win it.

This season has been unbelievable, so emotional, and when you do it like we did there are no words to describe how it happened. For all the club legends and fans who have waited so long I'm so, so happy. I want to win more. I'm hungry. This feeling is indescribable and I want to do it again...

Miracles do happen in Manchester but on this side of the road this time. It's one big blur for me, when the (final) goal went in. I just remember jumping on top of Sergio when he scored. He was crying on the floor, other guys were pouring their eyes out and I'm talking strong personalities who you don't see get emotional often. Then, all of a sudden, it was finished.

We're champions but it's not about coming here for money and all these stories we've heard. We've dreamed of this moment all of our lives, when we were kids, when we had no money, when we had nothing. Now we are the champions and that's all it's about. You see the fans and how happy they are. It's just unbelievable.'

PABLO ZABALETA:

'When we were losing 2-1, I thought, 'We'll score one goal and we're still going to lose.' I don't want to wake up from this. You just look at the players and the fans, everybody deserves this. The most important thing for any team is when you believe. If you believe in yourself you win. We believed until the last minute.'

'I DON'T WANT TO WAKE UP FROM THIS. YOU JUST LOOK AT THE PLAYERS AND THE FANS, EVERYBODY DESERVES THIS. THE MOST IMPORTANT THING FOR ANY TEAM IS WHEN YOU BELIEVE. IF YOU BELIEVE IN YOURSELF YOU WIN. WE BELIEVED UNTIL THE LAST MINUTE'

NIGEL DE JONG:

'If you can win an English Premier League title after such a crazy year and finish it off like this it is unbelievable. There are so many mixed emotions but to share it today with the fans and the families is a great moment.

I think we deserved it in the end. When we went 2-1 down, everyone around us was losing the faith but on the pitch we had to keep the faith and keep patient. Scoring two brilliant goals in the space of three minutes just changed the game.

The faith in the team and the belief in the team is just so strong. Everybody kept their focus and I think that's what made us stronger this season.

My main priority today (against QPR) was to prevent goals instead of scoring them. It didn't really quite work out but at the end of the day we got the three points and we're champions!'

'IF YOU CAN WIN AN ENGLISH PREMIER LEAGUE TITLE AFTER SUCH A CRAZY YEAR AND FINISH IT OFF LIKE THIS IT IS UNBELIEVABLE. THERE ARE SO MANY MIXED EMOTIONS BUT TO SHARE IT TODAY WITH THE FANS AND THE FAMILIES IS A GREAT MOMENT. I THINK WE DESERVED IT IN THE END. THE FAITH IN THE TEAM AND THE BELIEF IN THE TEAM IS JUST SO STRONG. EVERYBODY KEPT THEIR FOCUS'

GARETH BARRY:

'I WAS FEARING THE WORST WITH FIVE MINUTES TO GO. IT WAS A MASSIVE MOUNTAIN TO CLIMB. IT ALL FELL PERFECTLY, WITH QPR KNOWING THEY WERE SAFE AND ALL OF A SUDDEN WE WERE ON A HIGH'

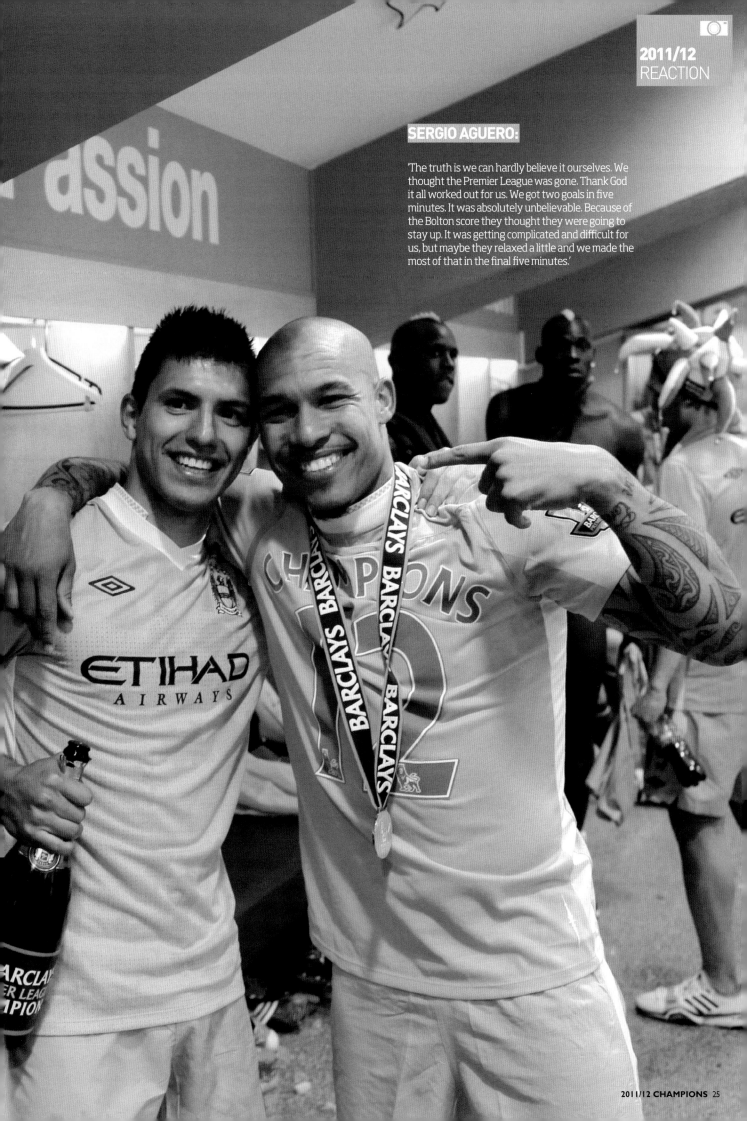

SERGIO AGUERO:

'The truth is we can hardly believe it ourselves. We thought the Premier League was gone. Thank God it all worked out for us. We got two goals in five minutes. It was absolutely unbelievable. Because of the Bolton score they thought they were going to stay up. It was getting complicated and difficult for us, but maybe they relaxed a little and we made the most of that in the final five minutes.'

MARIO BALOTELLI:

'We are the best and that's why we won. We didn't play very well in a few games but the rest of the season we played very well so we deserved to win. Personally I think too many people talked and too many people said bad things about me, and now they have to shut up! Manchester City is a great club, a great team and I have great team-mates. I don't see my future far from this club. I want to be here'

'WE ARE THE BEST AND THAT'S WHY WE WON. WE DIDN'T PLAY VERY WELL IN A FEW GAMES BUT THE REST OF THE SEASON WE PLAYED VERY WELL SO WE DESERVED TO WIN. I HAVE GREAT TEAM-MATES AND I DON'T SEE MY FUTURE FAR FROM THIS CLUB. I WANT TO BE HERE'

EDIN DZEKO:

'I'm happy that we won, we are champions and we deserve it, what a day! I don't know what to say. When the game started it was difficult because they played with ten players back. We scored the goal to put us 1-0 up but then we went down 2-1. There was still 25 minutes to go when the coach put me on. I said that I will do my best and try to change the game and then we did it. It was crazy because we scored two goals in two or three minutes. I'm so happy for these fans because they were amazing all season. To win it after so many years is amazing. I'm happy and proud to be part of this team'

'I'M HAPPY THAT WE WON, WE ARE CHAMPIONS AND WE DESERVE IT, WHAT A DAY! I DON'T KNOW WHAT TO SAY. I'M SO HAPPY FOR THESE FANS BECAUSE THEY WERE AMAZING ALL SEASON. TO WIN IT AFTER SO MANY YEARS IS AMAZING. I'M HAPPY AND PROUD TO BE PART OF THIS TEAM'

TASTE OF SUCCESS

Roberto Mancini kisses goodbye to 44 years and seals a new chapter in the club's history, sharing a special moment with the trophy after an emotional afternoon on the touchline

THE MANCINI

When Roberto Mancini was appointed the club's manager in December 2009, he arrived at the Etihad Stadium and immediately immersed himself in all things City. The blue and white scarf worn in most games may have appeared an affectation at first but it has come to be a symbol of the affection he feels for the club.

A stylish striker himself, who won Serie A with Sampdoria in 1990/91, Mancini admitted in an interview last year that he was "born to be a manager".

He explained: "I was a manager before I started to play football. I was always thinking like a manager. When I was young, I organised the teamsheet, where my friends would play. With Sven-Goran Eriksson (at Sampdoria and Lazio), I did the same.

Now I go back to my first love."

He articulated his approach to the job. "For me, working 24/7 is normal. To watch a match on TV, to study the opponent, is relaxation for me. Fabio Capello goes to the art gallery but he's 67. I'm 46 (47 now). Maybe in 20 years, I'll go to the art gallery. But when I'm here, I must work hard if we want to win. When we lose or draw, I think I am the guilty party. I made a mistake and want to know why."

History demonstrates he doesn't make many mistakes. His official managerial career began at Fiorentina in 2001. Despite the club being mired in financial trouble, he led them to the Coppa Italia before moving to Lazio in 2002. Once again resources were limited, but he landed another Coppa Italia and secured

Champions League qualification.

From there, it was on to Inter Milan in 2004 for a four-year reign that brought three successive Serie A titles before he was harshly dismissed in 2008. A subsequent contractual claim meant he couldn't take on another job until October 2009. Within weeks of a settlement, he was on his way to Manchester.

The Blues have been on an upward trajectory since he took over. After narrowly missing out on Champions League qualification in 2010, his first full season brought a third-place finish and a first major trophy since 1976. The FA Cup was won following a landmark semi-final defeat of Manchester United before Stoke were overcome in the final.

A goal-laden start to the 2011-12 campaign laid the foundations for the prize that was the all-consuming desire of every City supporter. It seems a long time since he was criticised for perceived conservatism in the initial stages of his stewardship.

All the time, he has been adding to the strength of the squad with astute purchases. Sergio Aguero, David Silva and Yaya Toure were recruited and, combined with Vincent Kompany and Joe Hart, have given the side a formidable spine.

For different reasons, there has been intense media focus on Carlos Tevez and Mario Balotelli this season but Mancini has been able to coax a series of significant perfor-

mances from both strikers. Without them, the wait for a league title may have stretched into a 45th year.

Far more often than not, he has made the right moves. In the decisive derby at the Etihad and six days later on Tyneside, he shifted Yaya Toure forward to great effect, preventing Manchester United from mounting a late cavalry charge and ensuring the Newcastle defence was breached so the Blues kept control of their own destiny going into the final weekend.

In the pre-match skirmishes, Mancini has always maintained control. His diplomacy has deflected the possibility of unwelcome distractions, defusing potential rows with his predecessor Mark Hughes ("a good manager") and Ferguson ("the best manager in the world") in the final week.

However, he has not shied away from standing up for the club when necessary. Many other managers have allowed respect for the Manchester United manager to become undue deference. When the Mancunian bosses went eyeball to eyeball at the Etihad on April 30, Mancini demonstrated that he would not be cowed by his rival's reputation and achievements. City fans love him for it.

In the interview in February last year, Mancini looked ahead and remarked: "I would like in 2013 all the City supporters to have a good memory of me and of the players that changed history."

Job done, with 12 months to spare.

Veni, vidi, vici: Our Italian boss soaks up the occasion, literally, with Dzeko and takes the rest of it in his stride

Roberto enjoys the moment with assistant manager Brian Kidd

MANCHESTER
MANCHESTER

SIX
OF THE BEST

THE MATCHES THAT HELPED DEFINE
THE TITLE-WINNING CAMPAIGN

All match reports **by NEIL JEFFRIES**
Stats compiled **by TREVOR HARTLEY**

MANCHESTER UTD 1
MANCHESTER CITY 6
Old Trafford, 23.10.11

6-1...

The most incredible derby result in living memory confirmed the shift in the balance of power in Manchester – and within English football – as City vanquished United 6-1.

Mario Balotelli opened the scoring before providing one of the most memorable moments of the season by unveiling his 'Why always me?' t-shirt.

Jonny Evans was shown a red card at the start of the second half and Mancini's men showed thrilling ruthlessness in tearing United apart.

First, James Milner crossed for Balotelli to convert his second after 59 minutes, before Sergio Aguero sent the travelling army into ecstasy with a composed finish.

Darren Fletcher pulled one back after 80 minutes but City were far from done. Incredibly, 3-1 became 6-1 within four mad minutes as Edin Dzeko (two) and David Silva ran riot in front of a rapidly emptying Old Trafford.

There had been magnificent performances all over the pitch with Balotelli, Silva and Vincent Company excelling, but it was the dynamism of Micah Richards who took the Man of the Match award.

The result left City five points clear at the top of the Barclays Premier League – but that fact was almost incidental.

MANCHESTER UNITED: De Gea, Smalling, Evans, Ferdinand, Evra, Nani (Hernandez 65), Anderson (Jones 66), Fletcher, Young, Rooney, Welbeck. Unused: Lindegaard, Fabio Da Silva, Park Ji-Sung, Valencia, Berbatov.

MANCHESTER CITY: Hart, Richards, Kompany, Lescott, Clichy, Barry, Yaya Toure, Milner (Kolarov 89), Silva, Balotelli (Dzeko 70), Aguero (Nasri 75). Unused: Pantilimon, Zabaleta, Kolo Toure, De Jong.

GOALS: Fletcher 81 (Manchester United); Balotelli 22, 60, Aguero 69, Dzeko 90, 90+3 Silva 90+1 (Manchester City).
SENT OFF: Evans 47.
REFEREE: M. Clattenburg.
ATTENDANCE: 75,487.

TEAM NEWS

■ There were six changes from the European game in midweek, but only two compared to the last Premier League game. Sergio Aguero and David Silva are the two who come into the side who had defeated Aston Villa the previous Saturday.

MATCH POINTS

■ City equalled the derby match scoring record by repeating the 6-1 scoreline at Old Trafford in 1926.
■ This was the Reds' biggest margin of defeat in a home game since going down 5-0 to Les McDowall's City team in 1955.
■ The last time United conceded six goals at home was in 1930 when, in the space of four days, they lost 6-0 to Huddersfield Town and 7-4 to Newcastle United.
■ United's defeat – their first at home since April 2010 – ended a run of 19 consecutive Premier League wins at Old Trafford.

SUPER MARIO

It was an afternoon of fluctuating fortunes as City and Tottenham Hotspur played out a breathless encounter with Mario Balotelli – who else? – having the final word.

In truth, the first period was forgettable but the second half exploded into life, with four goals in nine minutes as the two best footballing teams in the Premier League went all out for the win.

At the time, Spurs harboured genuine title ambitions – but this result went a long way to taking Harry Redknapp's men out of the equation.

The scoring began in the 56th minute when David Silva's wonderful pass sent Samir Nasri racing clear and he made no mistake, drilling past Brad Friedel.

Three minutes later it was 2-0 despite Joleon Lescott ending in the back of the net before the ball as he scrambled home Edin Dzeko's flick-on from a corner.

That ought to have been that but Stefan Savic's poor header allowed Jermain Defoe to pull one back within a minute, and the clock hands had barely moved again before Gareth Bale swept home a magnificent equaliser.

In stoppage time Jermain Defoe was inches away from reaching Bale's cross for a Spurs winner. However, City immediately went up the other end and won a penalty as Ledley King brought down Balotelli, who dusted himself down and coolly converted from 12 yards to send the ground into raptures.

MANCHESTER CITY: Hart, Richards, Savic, Lescott, Clichy, Milner, Barry, Silva, Aguero, Nasri, Dzeko (Balotelli 65). Unused: Pantilimon, Zabaleta, A Johnson, Kolarov, Onuoha, De Jong.

TOTTENHAM HOTSPUR: Friedel, Walker, Kaboul, King, Assou-Ekotto, Lennon (Pienaar 88), Parker, Modric, Van Der Vaart (Livermore 67), Bale, Defoe. Unused: Cudicini, Pavlyuchenko, Bassong, Dawson, Kranjcar.

GOALS: Nasri 56, Lescott 59, Balotelli 90 pen (Manchester City); Defoe 60, Bale 65 (Tottenham Hotspur).
REFEREE: H. Webb.
ATTENDANCE: 47,422.

TEAM NEWS

■ There was only the one change to the side – Micah Richards replacing Pablo Zabaleta – for what became one of the more crucial fixtures in recent times.

■ Substitute Mario Balotelli, having missed the previous three Premier League games, returned at a pivotal moment – brought down for a penalty and then scoring the injury-time winner.

MATCH POINTS

■ The 16th consecutive home league win equalled the 90-year-old club record – which was set between November 1920 and August 1921.

■ Another milestone was that it was the club's 200th win in the Premier League after 566 games.

SAMIR STRIKES LATE

City set a Premier League record and sent a powerful message to all their title rivals, coming from behind late in the game to defeat Chelsea.

It was a 20th consecutive home win for the Blues, who became only the fourth side in top-flight history to achieve the feat following Liverpool in 1972, Newcastle United in 1906-07 and Preston North End in 1891-92.

It was also the evening that Carlos Tevez returned to the City squad for the first time since September.

City were dominant in the first half but were unable to penetrate the Chelsea defence, who protected Petr Cech's goal admirably.

The home team continued to press but it was Chelsea, revived under Roberto Di Matteo's stewardship, who took the lead when Gary Cahill's deflected shot found the net following a corner.

Tevez was summoned from the bench but it was his Argentinean countryman Sergio Aguero who levelled the score from the penalty spot after Michael Essien had handled in the box.

Samir Nasri won the game five minutes from time with a neat finish after being put through by Tevez. The result meant City stayed within one point of United with nine games to play.

MANCHESTER CITY: Hart, Zabaleta, Richards, Kolo Toure, Clichy, De Jong (Tevez 66), Yaya Toure, Silva (Dzeko 76), Nasri, Aguero, Balotelli (Barry h-t). Unused: Pantilimon, Savic, Kolarov, Milner.

CHELSEA: Cech, Ivanovic (Bosingwa 21), Cahill, Luiz, Cole, Mikel, Lampard, Ramires, Meireles (Essien 58), Mata, Torres (Drogba 73). Unused: Turnbull, Malouda, Kalou, Sturridge.

GOALS: Aguero 78 pen, Nasri 85 (Manchester City); Cahill 60 (Chelsea).
REFEREE: M. Dean.
ATTENDANCE: 46,324.

TEAM NEWS

■ Roberto Mancini made four changes from the previous match against Sporting Lisbon in the Europa League.
■ Pablo Zabaleta was fit to return in a re-adjusted defence – but Vincent Kompany and Joleon Lescott were still unavailable.
■ Gael Clichy, Nigel De Jong and Samir Nasri were back in the starting XI and Gareth Barry was given a second-half stint in midfield.
■ When Carlos Tevez joined the action – with City a goal behind – he was making his first senior appearance in six months since the home Carling Cup game against Birmingham City in September

MATCH POINTS

■ City became the first side to win 20 home games in a row in the Premier League, and were now just one behind Liverpool's top-flight record of 21 consecutive home wins, set in 1972.

CARLOS' TREBLE

Carlos Tevez hit a hat-trick as City ruthlessly despatched Norwich for their second 6-1 away win of the season.

In the process the Blues moved to within two points of United at the Barclays Premier League summit. Sergio Aguero also scored twice as Norwich were swept aside again, having already lost 5-1 at the Etihad Stadium in December.

The hosts began well but City soon established a stranglehold, before unleashing their attacking potential in the second half.

The Argentinean strikeforce helped establish a 2-0 lead at half-time. A rasping shot from Tevez swerved and deceived John Ruddy, and his cute backheel set up Aguero, whose first-time shot gave the Canaries keeper no chance.

One of Paul Lambert's substitutions paid off on 51 when Joe Hart's punch fell invitingly for Andy Surman, who drove the ball home to set up an intriguing remainder of the game.

Yaya Toure replaced Samir Nasri as the half wore on, and he had a big say in the two goals that put the result beyond doubt. His shot was parried into the air by Ruddy, and Tevez rose to nod home. Within minutes Toure had fed Aguero, who sped towards the area before curling an exquisite shot into the far corner.

An under-hit backpass from Elliott Bennett gave Tevez the chance to bag a hat-trick, one he took with relish. Aguero and Adam Johnson hit the woodwork before the winger rewarded the travelling fans by adding a sixth in stoppage time.

NORWICH CITY: Ruddy, R Martin, R Bennett, Ward, Drury, E Bennett, Howson, Johnson (Hoolahan h-t), Pilkington (Surman h-t), Holt, Wilbraham (Morison 68). Unused: Steer, Jackson, Fox, Naughton.

MANCHESTER CITY: Hart, Zabaleta, Kompany, Lescott, Clichy, De Jong, Barry, Silva (A Johnson 76), Aguero, Nasri (Yaya Toure 63), Tevez (Richards 82). Unused: Pantilimon, Kolarov, Milner, Dzeko.

GOALS: Surman 51 (Norwich City); Tevez 18, 73, 80, Aguero 27, 75, A Johnson 90 (Manchester City).
REFEREE: C. Foy.
ATTENDANCE: 26,812.

TEAM NEWS
■ There was one change in the starting line-up – Pablo Zabaleta in for Micah Richards – while Yaya Toure was back, coming on as a sub in the second half.

MATCH POINTS
■ This was the first season that Manchester City had scored six (or more) goals in two games in a single top-flight campaign since 1937/38.
■ In that season there were four instances: 7-1 v West Bromwich Albion, 7-1 and 6-1 v Derby County, plus 6-2 v Leeds.
■ In another milestone for the club, this was the first time that three players had scored hat-tricks in a Premier League season.

MANCHESTER CITY 1
MANCHESTER UTD 0
Etihad Stadium, 30.04.12

NOISY NEIGHBOURS

On an evening of incredible tension at the Etihad, City claimed pole position in the title race as United were beaten for the second time this season thanks to a towering header by the magnificent Vincent Kompany.

As our official website described it, this was the mother of all derbies – the demolition derby, titanic, epic, landscape-changing, momentous, tumultuous, gripping, huge, colossal being just some of the scores of adjectives used to describe the game in the wall-to-wall build-up.

With three games to go, United led by three points but City had a superior goal difference. A win for either side was likely to prove decisive but a draw would have been sufficient for the visitors.

In truth, the match itself was lacking in quality but Roberto Mancini's men showed all the ambition as United paid the price for

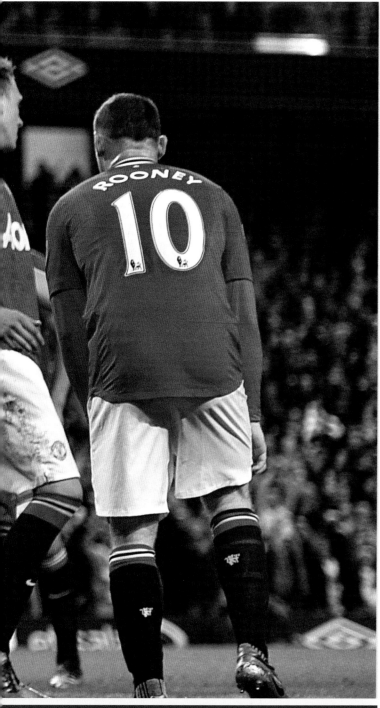

adopting a cautious, crabby approach.

In front of a raucous, seething, passionate crowd, United kept City at bay for almost all of the first half until Kompany rose to head home from David Silva's right-flank corner.

Yaya Toure was immense for City, breaking up United attacks and bursting forward himself whenever the opportunity arose. He, more than anyone else, ensured that City would seize the moment.

As nerves and sinews were stretched to breaking point in the final stages, the managers confronted each other on the touchline and, for City fans, it was extremely enjoyable to see Roberto Mancini refuse to yield an inch to his United counterpart.

The final whistle prompted scenes of jubilation in the stands and prompted a bullish Liam Gallagher to enter the media area and give an impromptu press conference to baffled but amused journalists.

As for the ultimate prize, it was now tantalisingly within City's reach – but two more games remained, and City could not afford any slip ups.

MANCHESTER CITY: Hart, Zabaleta, Kompany, Lescott, Clichy, Yaya Toure, Barry, Nasri (Milner 90), Tevez (De Jong 68), Silva (Richards 82), Aguero.
Unused: Pantilimon, Kolarov, Dzeko, Balotelli.

MANCHESTER UNITED: De Gea, Jones, Smalling, Ferdinand, Evra, Carrick, Scholes (Valencia 78), Nani (Young 83), Park Ji-Sung (Welbeck 58), Giggs, Rooney.
Unused: Amos, Berbatov, Rafael Da Silva, Hernandez.

GOAL: Kompany 45.
REFEREE: A. Marriner.
ATTENDANCE: 47,259.

TEAM NEWS

■ There were three changes from the previous match against Wolves, with City going into "the mother of all derbies" with eight of the players who started in the October win at Old Trafford.
■ Micah Richards, James Milner and Mario Balotelli were on the bench for the return meeting; coming into the team were Pablo Zabaleta, Samir Nasri and Carlos Tevez.

MATCH POINTS

■ Vincent Kompany's goal was City's first against United in a home Premier League game since Giovanni's winner in August 2007.
■ City's double was the first to be completed by the Blues in the derby since February 2008, when Darius Vassell and Benjani scored in a 2-1 win at Old Trafford.
■ The Blues' 26th win of the season equalled the number of victories achieved by the club's last title-winning team in 67/68.

YAYA DOUBLE

It took a while in coming but two goals in the last 20 minutes ensured City would go into the final weekend of the Barclays Premier League season at the summit.

Once again, Yaya Toure showed himself to be the man for the big occasion as he got both of them to edge out Champions League-chasing Newcastle United.

City's starting XI was the same for the third consecutive match, with Pablo Zabaleta keeping Micah Richards confined to the bench. The only change Roberto Mancini did make was to have Adam Johnson as one of his replacements rather than Mario Balotelli.

With so much at stake for both sides, it was no surprise that the opening spell was a cagey one. The hosts had the early ascendency with plenty of possession but they rarely troubled Joe Hart, while opposite number Tim Krul was called into action to make comfortable blocks to deny Samir Nasri and David Silva.

The Blues began to assert themselves and as the intensity increased, referee Howard Webb was kept busy, making five bookings within the space of 12 minutes.

City almost took the lead as half-time approached but Gareth Barry was denied by magnificent blocks from Fabricio Coloccini and Davide Santon.

The introduction of Nigel De Jong allowed Toure more freedom to get forward and the move paid off with 20 minutes to go when the man who has the happy knack of scoring key goals did it again. The Ivorian started and finished the move, feeding Sergio Aguero and latching on to the return, before curling the ball past Krul's left hand with a shot that oozed composure and class.

As the clock ran down, substitute Micah Richards made a crucial block to deny Shola Ameobi, before Toure popped up again to score the clincher after City broke forward from a Newcastle corner.

There were now 90 minutes (+5) of the season to go...

TEAM NEWS

■ City kept the same team for the third game in a row, while Newcastle were also unchanged from the team that achieved a midweek 2-0 win at Chelsea.

MATCH POINTS

■ The Sport Direct Arena was packed to capacity for a meeting of Champions League contenders and potential champions.
■ City chalked up the 27th league win of the season – one more than the total set by the club's last championship-winning team in 1968.
■ The goal difference advantage over United at the top of the table remained intact after 2-0 wins for both teams on the day, United having defeated Swansea City at Old Trafford.

THE REST OF THE STORY

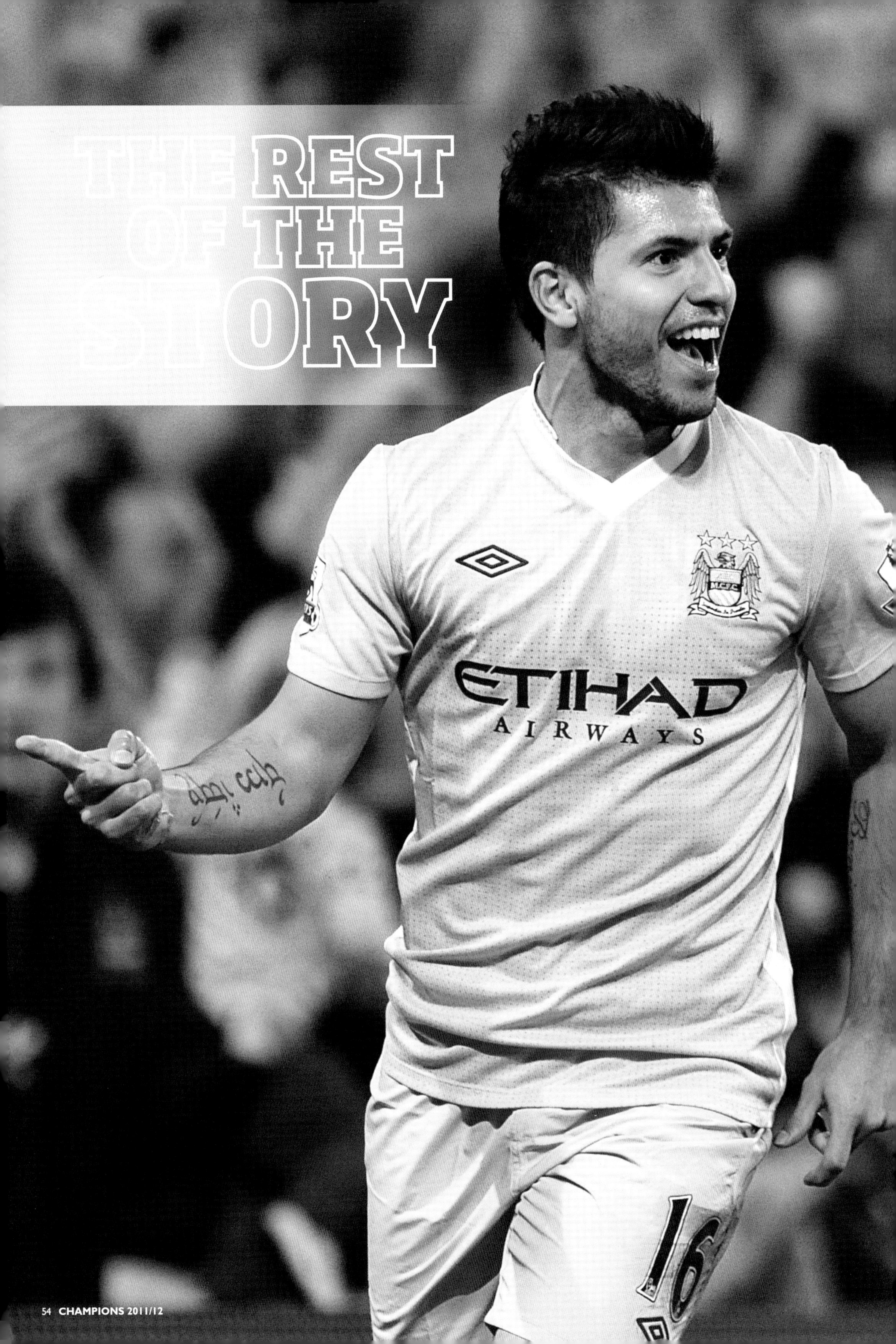

MANCHESTER CITY 4 SWANSEA CITY 0, Etihad Stadium, 15.08.11

TEAM NEWS

■ Eight of City's FA Cup final team were in the starting XI for the first game of the season. New signing Gael Clichy and Wembley subs Adam Johnson and Edin Dzeko were the three newcomers who came into the side.

■ Second-half subs, Sergio Aguero and Stefan Savic, made their first league appearances in England.

MATCH POINTS

■ Sergio Aguero was the first player in more than six years to score two goals on his Premier League debut. The last was Tottenham Hotspur's Egyptian striker, Mido, in a match against Portsmouth in February 2005.

■ Swansea City had now lost in their season opener for the sixth year in a row. They were at the third level of English football when they last took three points from their first match.

MANCHESTER CITY: Hart, Richards, Kompany, Lescott, Clichy, De Jong (Aguero 59), Barry, A Johnson (Savic 74), Yaya Toure, Silva (Milner 82), Dzeko. Unused: Taylor, Zabaleta, Kolarov, Balotelli.

SWANSEA CITY: Vorm, Rangel, Williams, Caulker, Tate, Dyer (Lita 81), Agustien, Britton (Allen 65), Sinclair, Dobbie (Routledge 65), Graham. Unused: Moreira, Orlandi, Gower, Moore.

GOALS: Dzeko 57, Aguero 68, 90, Silva 71.
ATTENDANCE: 46,802.

TEAM NEWS

■ A foot injury kept Nigel De Jong out, while two of the starters from the first match – Gael Clichy and Adam Johnson – reverted to the bench.
■ Sergio Aguero made his full league bow, while Aleksandar Kolarov and James Milner came in.
■ Carlos Tevez made his first appearance of the season, appearing as sub, while Costel Pantilimon was deputy keeper for the first time.

MATCH POINTS

■ City made it five wins in a row for the second time in the club's 15 Premier League seasons.
■ Seven goals in the first two games is the best scoring start for City in a top-flight campaign since 1961.

BOLTON WANDERERS: Jaaskelainen, Steinsson, Cahill, Knight, Robinson, Eagles (Pratley 78), Muamba (M Davies 59), Reo-Coker, Petrov, K Davies, Klasnic. Unused: Bogdan, Alonso, Blake, Wheater, Blakeman.

MANCHESTER CITY: Hart, Richards, Kompany, Lescott, Kolarov, Milner, Barry, Yaya Toure, Silva (Zabaleta 88), Dzeko (A Johnson 80), Aguero (Tevez 68). Unused: Pantilimon, Clichy, Savic, Balotelli.

GOALS: Klasnic 39, K Davies 63 (Bolton Wanderers); Silva 26 Barry 37 Dzeko 47 (Manchester City).
ATTENDANCE: 24,273.

TOTTENHAM HOTSPUR 1 MANCHESTER CITY 5, White Hart Lane, 28.08.11

TEAM NEWS

■ Samir Nasri was given an early debut. Pablo Zabaleta made his first start of the term and Gael Clichy returned at left-back. Micah Richards, Aleksandar Kolarov and James Milner missed out.
■ Spurs finished a man short with Rafael Van Der Vaart going off injured after 74 minutes.

MATCH POINTS

■ Edin Dzeko became the fourth City player to hit a league hat-trick in three years (Robinho, Carlos Tevez and Mario Balotelli are the others).
■ City registered their biggest away win at Spurs, and their first since April 2003.

TOTTENHAM HOTSPUR: Friedel, Corluka, Dawson, Kaboul, Assou-Ekotto, Lennon (Defoe 52), Modric (Livermore 66), Kranjcar (Huddlestone h-t), Bale, Van Der Vaart, Crouch. Unused: Cudicini, Walker, Bassong, Pavlyuchenko.

MANCHESTER CITY: Hart, Zabaleta (Richards 64), Kompany, Lescott, Clichy, Silva, Yaya Toure, Barry, Nasri, Aguero (Savic 75), Dzeko. Unused: Pantilimon, Milner, A Johnson, Tevez, Balotelli.

GOALS: Kaboul 68 (Tottenham Hotspur); Dzeko 34, 41, 55, 90, Aguero 60 (Manchester City).
ATTENDANCE: 36,150.

MANCHESTER CITY 3 WIGAN ATHLETIC 0, Etihad Stadium, 10.09.11

TEAM NEWS
■ With four games gone there were only five players who had started each one - Joe Hart, Vincent Kompany, Joleon Lescott, David Silva and Yaya Toure.
■ Last season's top scorer, Carlos Tevez, made his first start instead of the Premier League's leading marksman, Edin Dzeko.
■ Micah Richards, James Milner and Adam Johnson came into the team, with Pablo Zabaleta, Gareth Barry and Samir Nasri rested.
■ Kolo Toure was named on the bench - his first appearance in the Premier League squad since February.

MANCHESTER CITY: Hart, Richards, Kompany, Lescott, Clichy, Yaya Toure (Razak 80), Milner, Silva, Tevez (Nasri 60), Aguero (Balotelli 70), A Johnson. Unused: Pantilimon, Zabaleta, Kolo Toure, Dzeko.

WIGAN ATHLETIC: Al-Habsi, Lopez, Caldwell, Boyce (Stam 60), Figueroa, Watson (Gomez 70), Diame, McArthur, Moses, Di Santo (Crusat 70), Rodallega. Unused: Kirkland, Jones, Sammon, McCarthy.

GOALS: Aguero 13, 63, 69.
ATTENDANCE: 46,509.

FULHAM 2 MANCHESTER CITY 2, Craven Cottage, 18.09.11

TEAM NEWS
■ Regular league full-back pairing Micah Richards and Gael Clichy started. Pablo Zabaleta appeared in the second half, and Aleksandar Kolarov - none the worse for his broken nose sustained against Napoli - was on the bench.
■ The only other change in the squad was Mario Balotelli in for Stefan Savic.
MATCH POINTS
■ City's run of seven successive league wins came to an end two games short of the club's all-time league record set in 1912.
■ Danny Murphy had scored two Premier League goals in 18 months - both against City.

FULHAM: Schwarzer, Kelly, Baird, Hangeland, Riise, Duff (Kasami 61), Murphy, Sidwell, Dempsey, Zamora, Dembele (Ruiz 88). Unused: Etheridge, Orlando Sa, Senderos, Gecov, Grygera.

MANCHESTER CITY: Hart, Richards, Kompany, Lescott, Clichy, Yaya Toure, Barry, Silva (Zabaleta 69), Aguero (Tevez 82), Nasri (A Johnson 81), Dzeko. Unused: Pantilimon, Kolarov, Kolo Toure, Balotelli

GOALS: Zamora 55, Murphy 75 (Fulham); Aguero 18, 46 (Manchester City).
ATTENDANCE: 24,750.

TEAM NEWS
■ After the midweek rotation for Carling Cup action against Birmingham City, Mancini reverted to the line-up at Fulham. It was the first time the Blues had been unchanged in successive Premier League matches in 2011/12.

MATCH POINTS
■ Plaudits for Roberto Mancini's tactical changes as two of the subs grabbed the goals in the first home win against Everton since 2007.
■ James Milner's goal was his first in the Premier League in 58 weeks since he scored on his last appearance for Aston Villa in August 2010.

MANCHESTER CITY: Hart, Richards, Kompany, Lescott, Clichy, Yaya Toure, Barry, Nasri (Savic 83), Silva, Aguero (Milner 78), Dzeko (Balotelli 60). Unused: Pantilimon, Zabaleta, Kolarov, Tevez.

EVERTON: Howard, Hibbert, Jagielka, Distin, Baines, Coleman (Vellios 81), Neville (Drenthe 73), Rodwell, Osman, Fellaini, Cahill (Saha 66). Unused: Mucha, Heitinga, Bilyaletdinov, Stracqualursi.

GOALS: Balotelli 68, Milner 89.
ATTENDANCE: 47,293.

BLACKBURN ROVERS 0 MANCHESTER CITY 4, Ewood Park, 01.10.11

TEAM NEWS
■ Mario Balotelli made his first league start of the season.
■ Joleon Lescott was back to maintain an ever-present Premier League central defensive partnership with Vincent Kompany.
■ Pablo Zabaleta and Aleksandar Kolarov were recalled in the full-back roles and James Milner took over from Gareth Barry in midfield.
■ Adam Johnson came in for Samir Nasri.

MATCH POINTS
■ City made it eight league games unbeaten against Blackburn since 2007.
■ Samir Nasri and Stefan Savic scored their first Premier League goals for City.

BLACKBURN ROVERS: Robinson, Lowe, Samba, Dann, Givet, Petrovic, Goodwillie (Formica 61), Nzoni, Pedersen, Hoilett, Yakubu. Unused: Bunn, Slew, Rochina, Vukcevic, Roberts, Hanley.

MANCHESTER CITY: Hart, Zabaleta, Kompany, Lescott, Kolarov, Milner, Yaya Toure, A Johnson (Savic 79), Silva, Balotelli (Dzeko 88), Aguero (Nasri 27). Unused: Pantilimon, Barry, Clichy, De Jong.

GOALS: Johnson 56, Balotelli 59, Nasri 73, Savic 87.
ATTENDANCE: 24,760.

MANCHESTER CITY 4 ASTON VILLA 1, Etihad Stadium, 15.10.11

TEAM NEWS
■ Nigel De Jong, started for the first time since the opening game, and Gareth Barry resumed in midfield. David Silva and the injured Sergio Aguero were the two to make way.
■ The rotation of the full-backs continued with Micah Richards and Gael Clichy coming in.
■ Owen Hargreaves played in the league for the first time in almost a year, while Kolo Toure made a first league appearance since February.

MATCH POINTS
■ City went top after making it five home wins in a row.
■ Stephen Warnock's goal was the first scored past Joe Hart in a home league game since May.

MANCHESTER CITY: Hart, Richards (Kolo Toure 66), Kompany, Lescott, Clichy, De Jong, Barry, Milner, Yaya Toure (Silva 66), A Johnson (Hargreaves 77), Balotelli. Unused: Pantilimon, Kolarov, Nasri, Dzeko.

ASTON VILLA: Given, Hutton, Dunne, Clark, Warnock, Petrov, Delph (Albrighton 76), Ireland (N'Zogbia 55), Heskey (Bannan 63), Bent, Agbonlahor. Unused: Guzan, Cuellar, Herd, Weimann

GOALS: Balotelli 28, Johnson 47, Kompany 52, Milner 71 (Manchester City); Warnock 65 (Aston Villa).
ATTENDANCE: 47,019.

MANCHESTER CITY 3 WOLVERHAMPTON WANDERERS 1, Etihad Stadium, 29.10.11

TEAM NEWS
■ For the second meeting in four days, both managers rung the changes. Only three of the Carling Cup starters in the 5-2 victory were in City's team, and Wolves named just five from their midweek starting XI.

MATCH POINT
■ By beating Wolves at home for the third season in a row, City confirmed their position as the country's top-scoring team with 36 goals in 10 Premier League games.

MANCHESTER CITY: Hart, Richards, Kompany, Lescott, Kolarov, Yaya Toure, Barry, Nasri (Balotelli 71), Aguero (Savic 76), Silva, Dzeko (A Johnson 63). Unused: Pantilimon, Zabaleta, De Jong, Milner.

WOLVES: Hennessey, Stearman (Hammill 68), Johnson, Berra, Ward, Edwards, Henry, Guedioura (Ebanks–Blake 85), Hunt (Jarvis 85), O'Hara, Doyle. Unused: De Vries, Elokobi, Craddock, Vokes.

GOALS: Dzeko 51, Kolarov 67, Johnson 90 (Manchester City); Hunt 75 pen (Wolves).
SENT OFF: Kompany 74.
ATTENDANCE: 47,142.

TEAM NEWS

■ Micah Richards was named stand-in captain as Vincent Kompany served his one-match ban.
■ The team showed just two changes from the Premier League game against Wolves. Stefan Savic deputised for Kompany and James Milner came in for Samir Nasri.
■ Rangers included two City "old boys" in Joey Barton and Shaun Wright-Phillips.

MATCH POINTS

■ It proved a successful return to Loftus Road. It was City's first Premier League visit since 1995/96 – the season both clubs were relegated.
■ City became only the second team to win 10 of the first 11 games in a Premier League season.

QPR: Kenny, Young, Ferdinand, Gabbidon, Traore (Hill 90), Mackie (Smith 84), Faurlin, Barton, Wright-Phillips, Helguson, Bothroyd (Puncheon 76). Unused: Murphy, Orr, Derry, Andrade.

MANCHESTER CITY: Hart, Richards, Savic, Lescott, Kolarov, Yaya Toure, Barry (Balotelli 75), Milner, Aguero (A Johnson 68), Silva, Dzeko (Kolo Toure 88). Unused: Pantilimon, Zabaleta, Clichy, Nasri.

GOALS: Bothroyd 28, Helguson 69 (QPR); Dzeko 43, Silva 52, Yaya Toure 74 (Manchester City).

ATTENDANCE: 18,076.

MANCHESTER CITY 3 NEWCASTLE UNITED 1, Etihad Stadium, 19.11.11

TEAM NEWS

■ Vincent Kompany, resuming after his ban, took over from Stefan Savic, Gael Clichy came in and Sami Nasri returned after injury.
■ Edin Dzeko, Gareth Barry, Aleksandar Kolarov and David Silva were rested.

MATCH POINTS

■ The league's strongest attack (42 goals in 12 games) outgunned the strongest defence (Newcastle had conceded eight in 11 games).
■ The attendance was an Etihad Stadium record.
■ City were now the only unbeaten side in the Premier League, the best since the league began.
■ The Blues made it 11 home wins in a row – the club's best sequence at the top level since 1921.

MANCHESTER CITY: Hart, Richards, Kompany, Lescott, Clichy, De Jong, Yaya Toure (Barry 84), Milner, Nasri, Aguero (A Johnson 75), Balotelli (Silva 69). Unused: Pantilimon, Kolo Toure, Kolarov, Dzeko.

NEWCASTLE UNITED: Krul, Simpson, S Taylor, Coloccini, R Taylor, Ben Arfa (Lovenkrands 76), Guthrie, Cabaye (Perch 85), Gutierrez, Ba, Sa. Ameobi (Gosling 79). Unused: Elliot, Santon, Smith, Sh. Ameobi.

GOALS: Balotelli 41 pen, Richards 44, Aguero 72 pen (Manchester City); Gosling 89 (Newcastle United).

ATTENDANCE: 47,408.

LIVERPOOL 1 MANCHESTER CITY 1, Anfield, 27.11.11

TEAM NEWS

■ Five changes were made from the side that lined up at Napoli as Micah Richards, Gael Clichy, Gareth Barry, Samir Nasri and Sergio Aguero returned to the starting team.

■ Former City striker Craig Bellamy was not considered for selection by Liverpool because he was said to be "devastated" by the death of Wales manager Gary Speed earlier in the day. The teams duly observed a minute's silence before kick-off.

LIVERPOOL: Reina, Johnson, Skrtel, Agger, Jose Enrique, Lucas, Adam, Henderson, Downing, Kuyt (Carroll 84), Suarez. Unused: Doni, Carragher, Coates, Kelly, Spearing, Maxi Rodriguez.

MANCHESTER CITY: Hart, Richards, Kompany, Lescott, Clichy, Milner, Barry, Yaya Toure, Nasri (Balotelli 65), Silva (Kolo Toure 90), Aguero (Dzeko 83). Unused: Pantilimon, Zabaleta, De Jong, A Johnson.

GOALS: Lescott 33 og (Liverpool); Kompany 31 (Manchester City).
SENT OFF: Balotelli 83 (two yellow cards).
ATTENDANCE: 45,071.

MANCHESTER CITY 5 NORWICH CITY 1, Etihad Stadium, 03.12.11

TEAM NEWS

■ After the Carling Cup win at Arsenal, Roberto Mancini reverted to a more familiar line-up.

■ There were two changes from the Liverpool game, Kolo Toure made a first league start since February and Edin Dzeko replaced James Milner.

■ Joleon Lescott took a break after playing in the first 13 league games.

MATCH POINTS

■ It was now 12 home wins in a row in the Premier League and 24 without defeat.

■ Three weeks before Christmas, City already had three strikers in double figures.

MANCHESTER CITY: Hart, Richards, Kompany, Kolo Toure, Clichy, Yaya Toure, Barry, Nasri (A Johnson 69), Silva, Aguero (Balotelli 72), Dzeko (De Jong 82). Unused: Pantilimon, Lescott, Savic, Milner.

NORWICH CITY: Ruddy, Naughton, R Martin, Barnett, Tierney, Pilkington (Hoolahan 60), Crofts, B Johnson (Fox 77), Bennett (Holt 60), Surman, Morison. Unused: Rudd, Whitbread, Wilbraham, Jackson.

GOALS: Aguero 32, Nasri 51, Yaya Toure 68, Balotelli 88, A Johnson 90 (Manchester City); Morison 81 (Norwich City).
ATTENDANCE: 47,201.

TEAM NEWS

■ Three changes were made from the side that defeated Bayern Munich the previous Wednesday: Pablo Zabaleta, James Milner and Mario Balotelli came in for Stefan Savic, Samir Nasri and Edin Dzeko.

MATCH POINTS

■ It was the end of the unbeaten start to the season as a late penalty inflicted City's first Premier League defeat since going down at Everton in May 2011.

■ The killer blow, as so often in the past, was landed by Frank Lampard – scoring for the sixth time in his last 10 Premier League meetings with the Blues.

CHELSEA: Cech, Bosingwa, Ivanovic, Terry, Cole, Romeu, Sturridge (Mikel 88), Ramires, Meireles (Lampard 73), Mata (Malouda 84), Drogba. Unused: Turnbull, Ferreira, Kalou, Torres.

MANCHESTER CITY: Hart, Zabaleta, Kompany, Lescott (Dzeko 85), Clichy, Yaya Toure, Barry, Silva (De Jong 75), Milner, Aguero (Kolo Toure 64), Balotelli. Unused: Pantilimon, Savic, A Johnson, Nasri.

GOALS: Meireles 34, Lampard 83 pen (Chelsea); Balotelli 2 (Manchester City). SENT OFF: Clichy 83 (second yellow card). ATTENDANCE: 41,730.

MANCHESTER CITY 1 ARSENAL 0, Etihad Stadium, 18.12.11

TEAM NEWS

■ Former Gunners Kolo Toure and Samir Nasri were recalled but Gael Clichy missed a meeting with his old club because of suspension.

■ Joleon Lescott and James Milner were on the bench and Pablo Zabaleta moved to left-back to cover for Clichy. This cleared the way for Micah Richards to resume at right-back.

MATCH POINTS

■ It was the half-century up in 16 matches: the fastest scoring 50 in the top-flight since 1962.

■ A full 12 months without a home defeat was now guaranteed. The midweek Stoke game fell 24 hours after the anniversary of the last loss.

MANCHESTER CITY: Hart, Richards, Kompany, Kolo Toure, Zabaleta, Yaya Toure (De Jong 85), Barry, Silva, Nasri (Dzeko 85), Aguero, Balotelli (Milner 72). Unused: Pantilimon, Lescott, Savic, A Johnson.

ARSENAL: Szczesny, Djourou (Miquel 47), Mertesacker (Chamakh 82), Koscielny, Vermaelen, Song, Arteta, Walcott (Arshavin 69), Ramsey, Gervinho, Van Persie. Unused: Almunia, Rosicky, Frimpong, Benayoun.

GOAL: Silva 53. ATTENDANCE: 47,303.

MANCHESTER CITY 3 STOKE CITY 0, Etihad Stadium, 21.12.11

TEAM NEWS
■ Three changes were made from the win against Arsenal: Gael Clichy returned after his suspension, Joleon Lescott took up his role in the back four and Adam Johnson made his first league start since October. Pablo Zabaleta, Kolo Toure and Mario Balotelli switched to the bench.

MATCH POINTS
■ Roberto Mancini marked his second anniversary with two significant achievements: Undefeated at home – 26 wins, two draws – through the calendar year of 2011.
Top of the league on Christmas Day for the first time since 1929.
■ The boss said of the unbeaten year at home: "It is a good record, something about which we can be proud and shows we are improving."

MANCHESTER CITY: Hart, Richards (Savic 59), Kompany, Lescott, Clichy, Yaya Toure, Barry (Milner 83), A Johnson, Nasri, Silva (Balotelli 68), Aguero. Unused: Pantilimon, Zabaleta, Kolo Toure, De Jong.

STOKE CITY: Sorensen, Woodgate (Diao 80), Huth, Upson, Wilson, Palacios, Shotton, Walters, Whitehead, Jerome (Fuller 68), Jones (Pennant 74). Unused: Begovic, Delap, Etherington, Arismendi.

GOALS: Aguero 29, 54, Johnson 36.
ATTENDANCE: 46,321.

WEST BROMWICH ALBION 0 MANCHESTER CITY 0, The Hawthorns, 26.12.11

TEAM NEWS
■ There were four changes for a visit to the ground where Mario Balotelli hit his first goals in England to wrap up a win in November 2010.
■ Balotelli came in for Adam Johnson prior to a testing first 11 days in the new year.
■ With his African Cup of Nations departure imminent, Kolo Toure again started instead of Joleon Lescott. Pablo Zabaleta's recall gave Micah Richards longer to get over a niggling injury, while James Milner replaced Gareth Barry.

MATCH POINTS
■ City failed to score in the league for the first time in 24 games since defeat at Liverpool.
■ Albion's point was their first (in their sixth game) in a Premier League Boxing Day fixture.

WBA: Foster, Jones, Olsson, McAuley, Shorey, Thomas, Scharner, Mulumbu (Dorrans 80), Brunt, Long, Odemwingie (Reyes 88). Unused: Fulop, Dawson, Thorne, Cox, Fortune.

MANCHESTER CITY: Hart, Zabaleta, Kolo Toure, Kompany, Clichy, Milner (Dzeko 82), Yaya Toure, Nasri (Barry 59), Aguero (A Johnson 74), Silva, Balotelli. Unused: Pantilimon, Lescott, Savic, De Jong.

ATTENDANCE: 25,938.

TEAM NEWS

■ Fit-again Aleksandar Kolarov came back for his first start since November as Roberto Mancini made six changes.

■ Gael Clichy joined James Milner, Sergio Aguero and David Silva in taking a turn on the bench.

■ The others returning were Joleon Lescott, Adam Johnson, Edin Dzeko, Gareth Barry and Nigel De Jong. Micah Richards re-appeared as sub after missing the game at West Brom.

MATCH POINT

■ Sunderland may have changed managers but for City it was a repeat story in the North East. In 2010/11 Steve Bruce's team took three points thanks to an injury-time penalty and now new boss Martin O'Neill celebrated a late winner.

SUNDERLAND: Mignolet, Gardner, O'Shea, Brown (Kilgallon 26), Colback, Larsson, Cattermole, Vaughan (Elmohamady 82), McClean, Sessegnon, Bendtner (Ji Dong-Won 78). Unused: Carson, Meyler, Noble, Laing.

MANCHESTER CITY: Hart, Zabaleta, Kompany, Lescott, Kolarov (Richards 67), Barry, De Jong (Aguero h-t), A Johnson, Yaya Toure, Nasri (Silva 55), Dzeko. Unused: Pantilimon, Clichy, Savic, Milner.

GOAL: Ji Dong-Won 90.
ATTENDANCE: 40,625.

MANCHESTER CITY 3 LIVERPOOL 0, Etihad Stadium, 03.01.12

TEAM NEWS

■ Mindful of the heavy demands on the squad, Roberto Mancini again made six changes as City went into the second match in little more than 48 hours. Back in the starting team were Micah Richards - after his substitute outing at the Stadium of Light - Kolo Toure, James Milner, Gael Clichy, Sergio Aguero and David Silva.

MATCH POINT

■ In repeating the previous season's 3-0 win against Liverpool, City made it 15 home wins in a row in the league - now only one short of the club record set in the old First Division in 1921.

MANCHESTER CITY: Hart, Richards, Kolo Toure, Kompany, Clichy, Yaya Toure, Barry, Silva (Lescott 76), Aguero (A Johnson 71), Milner, Dzeko. Unused: Pantilimon, Zabaleta, Kolarov, Savic, De Jong.

LIVERPOOL: Reina, Johnson, Skrtel, Agger, Jose Enrique, Spearing, Kuyt (Bellamy 57), Henderson, Adam (Gerrard 57), Downing, Carroll. Unused: Doni, Carragher, Shelvey, Kelly.

GOALS: Aguero 10 Yaya Toure 33 Milner 75 pen.
SENT OFF: Barry 72 (two yellow cards).
ATTENDANCE: 47,131.

WIGAN ATHLETIC 0 MANCHESTER CITY 1, DW Stadium, 16.01.12

TEAM NEWS

■ Pablo Zabaleta, on his 27th birthday, was given the captaincy, taking over from the injured Micah Richards. Mario Balotelli was also unavailable and Edin Dzeko filled the vacancy by scoring his first goal since November.

■ In two other changes, Samir Nasri and David Silva replaced Adam Johnson and Nigel De Jong.

■ Sub Nedum Onuoha played in the league for the first time since May – when he made his last appearance in a season's loan at Sunderland.

MATCH POINT

■ City went past the 50-point mark in 21 games – making the Blues only the fifth club to have posted a half-century at this stage since three points for a win began in 1981.

WIGAN ATHLETIC: Al Habsi, Stam, Caldwell, Alcaraz, Figueroa, Crusat (Di Santo 68), McArthur (Watson 68), McCarthy, Gomez (McManaman 81), Moses, Rodallega. Unused: Pollitt, Gohouri, Boyce, Sammon.

MANCHESTER CITY: Hart, Zabaleta, Savic, Lescott, Clichy, Milner, Barry, Silva (Onuoha 81), Aguero (A Johnson 90), Nasri (De Jong 74), Dzeko. Unused: Pantilimon, Kolarov, Hargreaves, Rekik.

GOAL: Dzeko 22
ATTENDANCE: 16,026.

EVERTON 1 MANCHESTER CITY 0, Goodison Park, 31.01.12

TEAM NEWS

■ It was a visit to Merseyside for the second week in a row following the Carling Cup semi-final, second leg at Liverpool. Roberto Mancini welcomed back Vincent Kompany after the captain's suspension, with Gael Clichy, James Milner and Sergio Aguero also returning to the starting team.

MATCH POINT

■ The Everton stranglehold re-asserted itself on City. After stopping a run of home defeats with a win in September, City are kept waiting for a double over the Merseysiders. The last time the club achieved the feat was in 1981.

EVERTON: Howard, Neville, Hibbert, Heitinga, Baines, Donovan, Gibson, Fellaini, Drenthe (Baxter 78), Cahill, Stracqualursi (Vellios 88). Unused: Mucha, Duffy, Barkley, Forshaw, Gueye.

MANCHESTER CITY: Hart, Richards, Kompany, Lescott (Kolarov 68), Clichy, Milner (A Johnson 62), Barry (De Jong 86), Silva, Aguero, Nasri, Dzeko. Unused: Pantilimon, Savic, Razak, Zabaleta.

GOAL: Gibson 60.
ATTENDANCE: 29,856.

TEAM NEWS

■ Three changes were made from the midweek game at Goodison Park: Stefan Savic replaced Vincent Kompany, an injury cutting short the captain's return after suspension, and Adam Johnson and Aleksandar Kolarov came in for James Milner and Gael Clichy.

■ David Pizarro was given the briefest of introductions to the Premier League as a stoppage-time substitute.

MATCH POINT

■ City surpassed a 1921 milestone in chalking up a new club record with the 17th consecutive home win in league football.

MANCHESTER CITY: Hart, Richards, Savic, Lescott, Kolarov, Barry, A Johnson (Pizarro 90), Silva, Nasri (Milner 54), Aguero (De Jong 80), Dzeko. Unused: Pantilimon, Zabaleta, Clichy, Rekik.

FULHAM: Schwarzer, Kelly, Hangeland, Senderos (Riise 73), Baird, Duff, Murphy, Etuhu (Ruiz 68), Davies, Dembele (Gecov 85), Dempsey. Unused: Stockdale, Kasami, Hughes, Frei.

GOALS: Aguero 10 pen, Baird 30 og, Dzeko 72.
ATTENDANCE: 46,963.

ASTON VILLA 0 MANCHESTER CITY 1, Villa Park, 12.02.12

TEAM NEWS

■ Vincent Kompany returned after injury and in a second change in the defence, Pablo Zabaleta came in for Micah Richards.

■ James Milner was in the team on the day of his 300th league appearance while Nigel De Jong made his fifth league start of the season.

MATCH POINTS

■ Off the top of the table for just over 24 hours, City leapfrogged United with a first win at Villa Park since November 2006.

■ Joleon Lescott bagged the only goal – his fifth in 10 league meetings, split between Everton and City, with the club he supported as boy.

ASTON VILLA: Given, Hutton, Dunne (Baker 90), Collins, Cuellar, Heskey (N'Zogbia 69), Petrov, Gardner, Albrighton (Ireland 77), Keane, Bent. Unused: Guzan, Warnock, Bannan, Weimann.

MANCHESTER CITY: Hart, Zabaleta, Kompany, Lescott, Kolarov, Barry, De Jong, A Johnson (Nasri 84), Milner, Silva (Richards 90), Aguero (Dzeko 89). Unused: Pantilimon, Savic, Clichy, Pizarro.

GOAL: Lescott 63.
ATTENDANCE: 35,132.

MANCHESTER CITY 3 BLACKBURN ROVERS 0, Etihad Stadium, 25.02.12

TEAM NEWS

■ There were four changes after the side made Europa League progress against FC Porto: Pablo Zabaleta and Aleksandar Kolarov returned as full-backs; Adam Johnson and Mario Balotelli came in for Samir Nasri and Gareth Barry.

■ Yaya Toure made his first Premier League appearance since January 3, after missing five matches due to the Africa Cup of Nations.

MATCH POINTS

■ The record-breaking run at home was extended to 18 consecutive wins in the league – almost exactly a year since Fulham became the last visiting team to leave with a point.

■ Sergio Aguero's goal was City 100th home league goal against Blackburn.

MANCHESTER CITY: Hart, Zabaleta, Kompany, Lescott, Kolarov, De Jong, Yaya Toure (Milner 86), A Johnson (Pizarro 71), Silva, Aguero, Balotelli (Dzeko 79). Unused: Pantilimon, Richards, Clichy, Nasri.

BLACKBURN ROVERS: Robinson, Orr, Dann, Hanley, Martin Olsson, Hoilett, Formica (Rochina 69), Petrovic (Nzonzi 69), Pedersen, Yakubu, Marcus Olsson. Unused: Bunn, Modeste, Goodwillie, Vukcevic, Henley.

GOALS: Balotelli 30, Aguero 52, Dzeko 81.
ATTENDANCE: 40, 511.

MANCHESTER CITY 2 BOLTON WANDERERS 0, Etihad Stadium, 03.03.12

TEAM NEWS

■ The midweek internationals were a consideration in selection. Nigel De Jong was rested while Aleksandar Kolarov, David Silva and Sergio Aguero remained on the bench.

■ David Pizarro made his first start alongside Gael Clichy, Gareth Barry and Samir Nasri.

■ Roberto Mancini had fitness issues at right-back. Micah Richards was out after his return for England and Pablo Zabaleta had to go off early.

MATCH POINTS

■ A 19th consecutive home win equalled the Premier League best set by Manchester United.

■ It was now City's most successful season at home in the Premier League with most wins (14) and most goals (42).

MANCHESTER CITY: Hart, Zabaleta (Kolo Toure 19), Kompany, Lescott, Clichy, Pizarro (Dzeko 62), Yaya Toure, Barry, A Johnson, Balotelli, Nasri (Milner 84). Unused: Pantilimon, Kolarov, Silva, Aguero.

BOLTON WANDERERS: Bogdan, Steinsson, Wheater, Knight, Ricketts, Ream, M Davies, Pratley (Muamba 87), Reo-Coker, Miyaichi, Ngog. Unused: Jaaskelainen, Robinson, Eagles, Petrov, Klasnic, Sordell.

GOALS: Clichy 23, Balotelli 69.
ATTENDANCE: 47,219.

TEAM NEWS

■ Kolo Toure, captain in his first league start since the African Cup of Nations, and Stefan Savic were the centre-back partners following injuries to Vincent Kompany and Joleon Lescott.

■ Yaya Toure returned after his Europa League suspension, Micah Richards resumed in the back four, Samir Nasri came into midfield and Mario Balotelli was the main striker.

■ Aleksandar Kolarov, James Milner, Sergio Aguero and Edin Dzeko, all starters in the Europa League at Sporting Lisbon, were on the bench.

MATCH POINT

■ City were knocked off the top of the table after leading the way for five months.

■ Swansea's Scott Sinclair missed a penalty for the first time when Joe Hart made a fine save in the sixth minute.

SWANSEA CITY: Vorm, Rangel, Williams, Caulker, Taylor, Routledge (Monk 88), Britton, Allen, Sigurdsson, Sinclair, Graham (Moore 79). Unused: Tremmel, Tate, McEachran, Gower, Lita.

MANCHESTER CITY: Hart, Richards, Kolo Toure, Savic, Clichy, De Jong, Barry (Aguero 38), Silva (Dzeko 87), Yaya Toure, Nasri (A Johnson 85), Balotelli. Unused: Pantilimon, Kolarov, Milner, Pizarro.

GOAL: Moore 83.
ATTENDANCE: 20,510.

  STOKE CITY 1 MANCHESTER CITY 1, Britannia Stadium 24.03.12

TEAM NEWS

■ An injury to Sergio Aguero created a starting place for Edin Dzeko and Gareth Barry, a half-time substitute in the 2-1 victory over Chelsea, was restored to the team, with Nigel De Jong going onto the bench.

MATCH POINT

■ Stoke continue to be a tough nut for City on their own patch. Since their promotion in 2008, they and the Blues have had five league and cup meetings, but City have yet to win there with a record of three draws and two defeats.

STOKE CITY: Begovic, Wilkinson, Shawcross, Huth, Wilson, Jerome (Pennant 51), Whelan, Whitehead, Etherington (Palacios 81), Walters, Crouch (Jones 90). Unused: Sorensen, Upson, Delap, Shotton.

MANCHESTER CITY: Hart, Zabaleta (Milner 84), Richards, Kolo Toure, Clichy, Yaya Toure, Barry (Tevez 74), Silva (A Johnson 72), Balotelli, Nasri, Dzeko. Unused: Pantilimon, Kolarov, Savic, De Jong.

GOALS: Crouch 59 (Stoke City); Yaya Toure 76 (Manchester City).
ATTENDANCE: 27,535.

MANCHESTER CITY 3 SUNDERLAND 3, Etihad Stadium, 31.03.12

TEAM NEWS

■ Vincent Kompany's return allowed Micah Richards to move to right-back while Aleksandar Kolarov came in for Gael Clichy on the left.

■ In two other alterations, the midfield was re-shaped with James Milner and Nigel De Jong in for Samir Nasri and Gareth Barry.

MATCH POINTS

■ Trailing at half-time for the first time in the league this term, City mount a stirring comeback – but the run of 20 successive home wins ends one short of Liverpool's top-flight record.

■ With the total of goals rising to 75, this is the club's best scoring season in the Premier League.

MANCHESTER CITY: Hart, Richards (A Johnson h-t), Kolo Toure, Kompany, Kolarov, De Jong, Yaya Toure, Milner (Pizarro 81), Balotelli, Silva (Tevez 58), Dzeko. Unused: Pantilimon, Zabaleta, Clichy, Barry.

SUNDERLAND: Mignolet, Bardsley, Turner, Kilgallon (Kyrgiakos 81), Colback, Larsson, Gardner, Cattermole (Vaughan 90), McClean, Sessegnon, Bendtner. Unused: Westwood, Richardson, Meyler, Ji Dong-Won, Campbell.

GOALS: Balotelli 43 pen, 85, Kolarov 86 (Manchester City); Larsson 31, 55, Bendtner 45 (Sunderland).

ATTENDANCE: 47,000.

ARSENAL 1 MANCHESTER CITY 0, Emirates Stadium, 08.04.12

TEAM NEWS

■ A knee injury kept David Silva out as Roberto Mancini shuffled his team with six changes.

■ Joleon Lescott was fit to start after a month's absence, Pablo Zabaleta and Gael Clichy returned as the full-backs, Gareth Barry and Samir Nasri were back in midfield and Sergio Aguero recovered from his recent injury.

MATCH POINT

■ Highbury or the Emirates – it's all the same when it comes to trying to win a league game at Arsenal. City may have been successful in the Carling Cup but it's now 37 years since the Blues won in the top-flight – on 4th October, 1975.

ARSENAL: Szczesny, Sagna, Koscielny, Vermaelen, Gibbs (Santos 56), Song, Walcott (Oxlade-Chamberlain 85), Rosicky, Arteta, Benayoun (Ramsey 78), Van Persie. Unused: Fabianski, Djourou, Jenkinson, Chamakh.

MANCHESTER CITY: Hart, Zabaleta, Kompany, Lescott, Clichy, Barry, Yaya Toure (Pizarro 17), Milner, Aguero (Tevez 83), Nasri (Kolarov 79), Balotelli. Unused: Pantilimon, Richards, De Jong, Dzeko.

GOAL: Arteta 87.

SENT OFF: Balotelli 90 (two yellow cards).

ATTENDANCE: 60,096.

TEAM NEWS

■ With Mario Balotelli serving a suspension, Carlos Tevez made his first start since returning to the squad – and scored a goal.

■ Micah Richards was back for Pablo Zabaleta, while Nigel De Jong and David Silva returned in midfield, with James Milner reverting to the bench and Yaya Toure on the injured list.

MATCH POINT

■ With their team showing five changes, Albion suffered their biggest defeat since Roy Hodgson was appointed as the Baggies' manager 14 months previously.

MANCHESTER CITY: Hart, Richards, Kompany, Lescott, Clichy, De Jong, Barry, Silva (Zabaleta 81), Aguero (Dzeko 74), Nasri, Tevez (A Johnson 63). Unused: Pantilimon, Kolarov, Milner, Pizarro.

WBA: Foster, Jones, Dawson, Olsson, Shorey, Cox, Andrews, Mulumbu (Fortune 68), Scharner, Dorrans (Tchoyi 78), Long. Unused: Daniels, McAuley, Odemwingie, Hurst, Roofe.

GOALS: Aguero 6, 54, Tevez 61, Silva 64.
ATTENDANCE: 46,746.

WOLVERHAMPTON WANDERERS 0 MANCHESTER CITY 2, Molineux, 22.04.12

TEAM NEWS

■ Roberto Mancini made only one change from the side that won convincingly at Norwich City eight days before. Yaya Toure, who had come on as a sub at Carrow Road, was restored to the starting XI with Nigel De Jong on the bench.

■ One other alteration saw Kolo Toure replace Micah Richards (hamstring) as substitute.

MATCH POINT

■ Victory meant City, who had been eight points behind with six games left, moved three points behind United, ahead of the derby.

■ The home defeat, a club record ninth successive loss at Molineux, meant relegation was confirmed for Wolves.

WOLVES: De Vries, Foley, Stearman, Bassong, Ward, Davis, Edwards (Doyle 61), Henry, Jarvis, Kightly, Fletcher (Ebanks-Blake 76). Unused: Ikeme, Johnson, Berra, Zubar, Milijas.

MANCHESTER CITY: Hart, Zabaleta, Kompany, Lescott, Clichy, Yaya Toure, Barry, Silva (De Jong 59), Aguero, Nasri (Kolo Toure 85), Tevez (A Johnson 74). Unused: Pantilimon, Kolarov, Milner, Dzeko.

GOALS: Aguero 27, Nasri 74.
ATTENDANCE: 24,576.

Our Moment in Time

 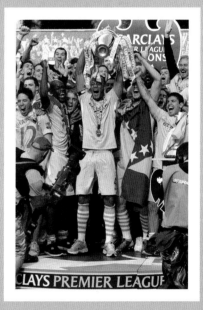

This is a chance to own a piece of history for your own home!

In commemoration of City's triumph on Sunday, MCFC charities are offering two iconic, framed and mounted prints of City's Premier League winning celebrations.

The exclusive, stunning prints framed and mounted in black may be purchased by emailing Lorraine.firth@mcfc.co.uk . The prints cost £75 and all proceeds will be donated to City in the Community programmes, supporting young people and their families in Manchester.

The prints are available for collection only from City@home.

FIRST DIVISION CHAMPIONS

1968

Lee-thal: Francis Lee is hailed by the City faithful after scoring the fourth against Newcastle United

"Never in league history can a season have moved towards such a breathtaking close"

If you needed any more proof that City never do things the easy way, then look to the team's final game of the 1967/68 season.

The Daily Mirror preview to the football fixtures on Saturday, May 11, 1968, set the scene nicely: "Never in League history can a season have moved towards such a breathtaking close.

"Newcastle stand between Manchester City and the title they could take from Manchester United. United, home to Sunderland, know that victory will not be enough if City succeed."

Just like the last match of 2011/12, this final fixture of the season was a cliff-hanger. Going into the game, manager Joe Mercer's charges were ahead of United on goal difference and needing a victory at St James' Park. However, in the background, both clubs faced the threat of being leapfrogged by Bill Shankly's Liverpool, who were three points behind and had a match in hand. (This was in the days of two points for a win).

An estimated 20,000 City fans travelled to the North East, and what a game they got. The Magpies started strongly, but City struck the first blow in the 14th minute when Mike Summerbee finished off a low, driven cross from Mike Doyle at the near post.

The relief of City's fans turned to angst in an instant, though, as Bryan "Pop" Robson put the ball past keeper Ken Mulhearn with the outside of his right boot.

It was an enthralling, open game, but the next decisive strike wouldn't come until just five minutes before half-time, when Neil Young met the ball on the turn at the edge of the box and smashed it home. Again, City's joy was tempered within seconds, as Jackie Sinclair put away a wonderful dipping shot over Mulhearn into the top far corner.

After the break, City piled on the pressure and got themselves into the lead for a third time, courtesy of Young once more. The Blues doubled their advantage just past the hour mark when, after a midfield battle, the ball was delivered to Colin Bell. His sublime reverse ball found Francis Lee charging into the box and the forward was at his sharpest, placing the ball beyond Willie McFaul.

Lee barely broke stride after the strike as he peeled off and ran towards the jubilant away fans.

Those supporters would have to endure a tense last few minutes after John McNamee put away a powerful header to make it 4-3. However, once the final whistle went, celebrating City players were swamped by equally ecstatic followers who had run onto the pitch.

City had won the title off their own steam, and it barely mattered that United's chance had faded with a 2-1 at the hands of Sunderland.

Jumping for joy: Neil Young celebrates finding the net against the Magpies

Jubilation: Fans run onto the pitch at St James' Park after the final whistle

Lighting up the City: Manager
Joe Mercer enjoys a cigar with
assistant manager Malcolm Allison

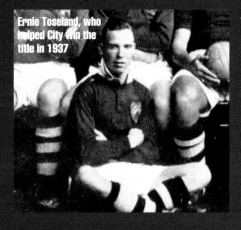

Ernie Toseland, who
helped City win the
title in 1937

FIRST DIVISION CHAMPIONS
1937

It was a tale of two cities when the Sky Blues clinched their first top-flight title in 1937, as rivals Manchester United were relegated to the Second Division.

Manager Wilf Wild's side were long considered a good outfit, having lifted the FA Cup in 1934, but the dominant team of the 1930s were north London's Arsenal.

City's season started off in a steady fashion, including a 6-2 win over West Bromwich Albion in September 1936, but they were sitting 10th by the end of the year. However, from Christmas, the team became invincible in the league – including a 1-0 win over United in January 1937 – and went on a run which saw them and Arsenal settle into the top two positions by the time the pair met that April.

This crunch tie sealed City's belief that they could go the whole way. In front of a record 74,918, City showed no mercy as Northern Irishman Peter Doherty and "flying winger" Ernie Toseland scored to secure a vital 2-0 win.

The riveting contest was summed up by a match report in the Daily Mirror: "A great game between two great sides. Arsenal at their most subtle and polished; City grand in spirit and brilliant in defence."

Wild's men had gone top with four games left, and never relinquished the spot. Arsenal eventually finished third, behind Charlton Athletic.

City had put away 107 goals that season, the only team to break a ton and, this time, the Daily Mirror gave a rather more matter-of-fact summary of the Citizens' achievement in April 1937: "So Manchester City have done it. Unbeaten run since Christmas Day and champions for the first time in history."

A more flowery appraisal appeared in the form of the Fletcher & Son poem, "Manchester City: Coronation year champions, 1937", the first letter on every line spelling out: "First Division Champions."

Netting the title: The ball
settles in the back of the
goal after Francis Lee
doubles City's lead

Manchester City Season 2011-12

Fixtures, dates and times are subject to change

Key: Played · Sub GS75 Sub used + initials of player replaced/time · Unused Sub Unused sub · 1 Goals scored · X Replaced · Debut City Debut · Yellow card ■ Red card

#					Opponent	F-A	Att	Pos	Away Fans	City scorers and goal times
1	Aug	Sun	7	W	Manchester U (FA Community Shield)	2-3	77,169	–	–	Lescott 38, Dzeko 45
2		Mon	15	H	**Swansea City**	4-0	46,802	2	2,785	Dzeko 57, Aguero 68, 90, Silva 71
3		Sun	21	A	Bolton Wanderers	3-2	24,273	1	4,846	Silva 26, Barry 37, Dzeko 47
4		Sun	28	A	Tottenham Hotspur	5-1	36,150	2	1,757	Dzeko 34, 41, 55, 90, Aguero 60
5	Sep	Sat	10	H	**Wigan Athletic**	3-0	46,509	2	1,122	Aguero 13, 63, 69
6		Wed	14	H	**Napoli** (UEFA Champions League)	1-1	44,026	–	2,533	Kolarov 75
7		Sun	18	A	Fulham	2-2	24,750	2	1,584	Aguero 18, 46
8		Wed	21	H	**Birmingham City** (Carling Cup 3)	2-0	25,070	–	494	Hargreaves 17, Balotelli 38
9		Sat	24	H	**Everton**	2-0	47,293	2	2,826	Balotelli 68, Milner 89
10		Tue	27	A	Bayern Munich (UEFA Champions League)	0-2	66,000	–	2,905	–
11	Oct	Sat	1	A	Blackburn Rovers	4-0	24,760	2	7,531	Johnson 56, Balotelli 59, Nasri 73, Savic 87
12		Sat	15	H	**Aston Villa**	4-1	47,019	1	1,528	Balotelli 28, Johnson 47, Kompany 52, Milner 71
13		Tue	18	H	**Villarreal** (UEFA Champions League)	2-1	42,236	–	91	Marchena og 43, Aguero 90+3
14		Sun	23	A	Manchester United	6-1	75,487	1	2,996	Balotelli 22, 60, Aguero 69, Dzeko 90, 90+3, Silva 90+1
15		Wed	26	A	Wolverhampton W (Carling Cup 4)	5-2	12,436	–	2,364	Johnson 37, Nasri 39, Dzeko 40, 64, Scapuzzi 50
16		Sat	29	H	**Wolverhampton Wanderers**	3-1	47,142	1	1,597	Dzeko 51, Kolarov 67, Johnson 90
17	Nov	Wed	2	A	Villarreal (UEFA Champions League)	3-0	24,235	–	1,611	Yaya Toure 30, 71, Balotelli pen 45
18		Sat	5	A	Queens Park Rangers	3-2	18,076	1	3,026	Dzeko 43, Silva 52, Yaya Toure 74
19		Sat	19	H	**Newcastle United**	3-1	47,408	1	1,685	Balotelli pen 41, Richards 44, Aguero pen 72
20		Tue	22	A	Napoli (UEFA Champions League)	1-2	57,575	–	1,072	Balotelli 33
21		Sun	27	A	Liverpool	1-1	45,071	1	2,964	Kompany 31
22		Tue	29	A	Arsenal (Carling Cup 5)	1-0	60,028	–	5,226	Aguero 83
23	Dec	Sat	3	H	**Norwich City**	5-1	47,201	1	2,786	Aguero 32, Nasri 51, Yaya Toure 68, Balotelli 88, A Johnson 90
24		Wed	7	H	**Bayern Munich** (UEFA Champions League)	2-0	46,002	–	2,623	Silva 37, Yaya Toure 52
25		Mon	12	A	Chelsea	1-2	41,730	1	1,458	Balotelli 2
26		Sun	18	H	**Arsenal**	1-0	47,303	1	2,796	Silva 53
27		Wed	21	H	**Stoke City**	3-0	46,321	1	853	Aguero 29, 54, A Johnson 36
28		Mon	26	A	West Bromwich Albion	0-0	25,938	1	2,560	–
29	Jan	Sun	1	A	Sunderland	0-1	40,625	1	2,101	–
30		Tue	3	H	**Liverpool**	3-0	47,131	1	2,685	Aguero 10, Yaya Toure 33, Milner pen 75
31		Sun	8	H	**Manchester United** (FA Cup 3)	2-3	46,808	–	5,961	Kolarov 48, Aguero 65
32		Wed	11	H	**Liverpool** (Carling Cup SF 1st leg)	0-1	36,017	–	5,850	–
33		Mon	16	A	Wigan Athletic	1-0	16,026	1	4,406	Dzeko 22
34		Sun	22	H	**Tottenham Hotspur**	3-2	47,422	1	2,804	Nasri 56, Lescott 59, Balotelli pen 90
35		Wed	25	A	Liverpool (Carling Cup SF 2nd leg)	2-2	44,590	–	6,131	De Jong 31, Dzeko 67
36		Tue	31	A	Everton	0-1	29,856	1	2,485	–
37	Feb	Sat	4	H	**Fulham**	3-0	46,963	1	741	Aguero pen 10, Baird og 30, Dzeko 72
38		Sun	12	A	Aston Villa	1-0	35,132	1	2,863	Lescott 63
39		Thu	16	A	Porto (Europa League R32 1st Leg)	2-1	47,417	–	1,350	Alvaro Pereira og 55, Aguero 84
40		Wed	22	H	**Porto** (Europa League R32 2nd Leg)	4-0	39,538	–	1,171	Aguero 1, Dzeko 76, Silva 84, Pizarro 86
41		Sat	25	H	**Blackburn Rovers**	3-0	46,782	1	556	Balotelli 30, Aguero 52, Dzeko 81
42	Mar	Sat	3	H	**Bolton Wanderers**	2-0	47,219	1	963	Clichy 23, Balotelli 69
43		Thu	8	A	Sporting Lisbon (Europa League R16 1st Leg)	0-1	34,371	–	878	–
44		Sun	11	A	Swansea City	0-1	20,510	2	2,032	–
45		Thu	15	H	**Sporting Lisbon** (Europa League R16 2nd Leg)	3-2	38,021	–	640	Aguero 60, 82, Balotelli pen 75
46		Wed	21	H	**Chelsea**	2-1	46,324	2	929	Aguero pen 78, Nasri 85
47		Sat	24	A	Stoke City	1-1	27,535	1	2,859	Yaya Toure 76
48		Sat	31	H	**Sunderland**	3-3	47,000	2	1,384	Balotelli 43 pen, 85, Kolarov 86
49	Apr	Sun	8	A	Arsenal	0-1	60,096	2	2,948	–
50		Wed	11	H	**West Bromwich Albion**	4-0	46,746	2	957	Aguero 6, 54, Tevez 61, Silva 64
51		Sat	14	A	Norwich City	6-1	26,812	2	2,439	Tevez 18, 73, 80, Aguero 27, 75, Johnson 90
52		Sun	22	A	Wolverhampton Wanderers	2-0	24,576	2	2,508	Aguero 27, Nasri 74
53		Mon	30	H	**Manchester United**	1-0	47,259	2	2,620	Kompany 45
54	May	Sun	6	A	Newcastle United	2-0	52,389	1	3,176	Yaya Toure 70, 89
55		Sun	13	H	**Queens Park Rangers**	3-2	47,435	1	2,778	Zabaleta 39, Dzeko 90+1, Aguero 90+3

#	Joe HART	Micah RICHARDS	Joleon LESCOTT	Vincent KOMPANY	Aleksandar KOLAROV	Nigel DE JONG	Yaya TOURE	James MILNER	David SILVA	Edin DZEKO	Mario BALOTELLI	Gareth BARRY	Adam JOHNSON	Gael CLICHY	Stuart TAYLOR	Stefan SAVIC	Sergio AGUERO	Pablo ZABALETA	Carlos TEVEZ	Costel PANTILIMON	Samir NASRI	Abdul RAZAK	Kolo TOURE	Nedum ONUOHA	Wayne BRIDGE	Owen HARGREAVES	Karim REKIK	Luca SCAPUZZI	Denis SUAREZ	David PIZARRO	Joan ROMAN
*1		1		X				X		1	X	Sub MB59	Sub JM67	Debut AK73	Unused Sub	Unused Sub	Unused Sub														
2			Unused Sub	X			Sub DS82		1 x	1	Unused Sub	X		Debut AJ74	Debut ND59	2	Unused Sub														
3									1 x	1 x	Unused Sub	1	Sub ED80	Unused Sub		Unused Sub	X	Sub DS88	Sub SA68	Unused Sub											
4	Sub PZ64						X		Unused Sub	4	Unused Sub		Unused Sub		Sub SA75	1 x	X	Unused Sub	Unused Sub	Debut											
5							X				Unused Sub	Sub SA70				3 x	Unused Sub	X	Unused Sub	Sub CT60	Sub YT80	Unused Sub									
6	Unused Sub			1 x			Unused Sub			X			Sub SN75	Sub AK75	Unused Sub			Sub ED81	Unused Sub		Unused Sub										
7					Unused Sub				X		Unused Sub		Sub SN81			2 x	Sub DS69	Sub SA82	Debut		Unused Sub										
8							Sub OH57				1				Unused Sub	Unused Sub	Unused Sub			Debut 1 x	X		X			Debut WB78	Debut AR86	Debut	Unused Sub		
9				Unused Sub				Sub SA78 1	X		Sub ED60 1	X			Sub SN83	X	Unused Sub	Unused Sub	Unused Sub	X											
10		Unused Sub		Sub GB73	Sub ED55			Sub SN69	X					Unused Sub		Unused Sub	Unused Sub	Unused Sub	X												
11				Unused Sub				Sub MB88	1 x	Unused Sub	1 x	Unused Sub		Sub AJ79 1				Unused Sub	Sub SA27 1												
12	X		1	Unused Sub		X		1	Sub YT66	Unused Sub	1		1 x				X	Unused Sub	Unused Sub		Unused Sub		Sub MR66			Sub AJ77					
13	Unused Sub			X				Sub SN81			Sub AJ40		Unused Sub		Unused Sub		Sub NDJ62 1		Unused Sub		Unused Sub										
14			Sub JM89	Unused Sub			X	1	Sub MB70 2	2 x						1 x	Unused Sub	Unused Sub	Sub SA75	Unused Sub											
15				Sub AR85				2	Unused Sub		1	Unused Sub							1 x	X	Unused Sub	Unused Sub		Sub LS73	1 x	Debut SN67					
16		■	1	Unused Sub		Unused Sub		1 x	Sub SN71	Sub ED63 1	Sub SA76			Unused Sub	Unused Sub																
17		Unused Sub	Sub MB82	2 x		X		Unused Sub	1 x	Unused Sub	Sub DS65		Sub YT74		Unused Sub																
18			1			1	1 x		Sub GB75		Sub SA68	Unused Sub	X		Unused Sub	Unused Sub			Sub ED88												
19	1		Unused Sub	X		Sub MB69	Unused Sub	1 x	Sub YT84	Sub SA75	Unused Sub		1 x		Unused Sub		Unused Sub														
20			X					1	Sub PZ85	Unused Sub		Unused Sub	Sub ED81	X		X	Unused Sub	Sub NDJ70													
21		1	Unused Sub			X	Sub SA83	Sub SN65 ■	Unused Sub		Unused Sub			X	Unused Sub	X	Sub DS90														
22	Unused Sub								1 x	Sub AK32 1		Unused Sub	Sub OH79					Unused Sub	Unused Sub		Unused Sub										
23		Unused Sub	Sub ED82	1	Unused Sub		X	Sub SA72 1	Sub SN69 1		Unused Sub	1 x	Unused Sub	1 x																	
24		Sub ED77	1 x	Unused Sub	1 x	X	Sub YT81		Sub DS84		Unused Sub	Unused Sub																			
25	X	Sub DS75		X	Sub JL85	1		Unused Sub ■		Unused Sub	X	Unused Sub	Sub SA64																		
26	Unused Sub	Sub YT85	Sub MB72	1	Sub SN85	X		Unused Sub		Unused Sub	X																				
27	X	Unused Sub	Sub GB83		Sub DS68	1		Sub MR59	2	Unused Sub	Unused Sub																				
28	Unused Sub	Unused Sub	X		Sub JM82	Sub SN59	Sub SA74		Unused Sub	Unused Sub	X																				
29	Sub AK67	X	X	Unused Sub	Sub SN55			Unused Sub	Unused Sub	Sub NDJ45	Unused Sub	X																			
30	Sub DS76	Unused Sub	Unused Sub	1	1		■	Sub SA71		Unused Sub	Unused Sub		Unused Sub																		
31	Unused Sub	■	1		X				X		Sub DS45	1	Sub AJ45		X	Unused Sub		Sub SN82			Unused Sub										
32	Sub SA72	Unused Sub	Sub SN74		Sub AJ66	X		1			X	Unused Sub		Unused Sub	Sub MB39			Unused Sub	Unused Sub												
33	Unused Sub	Sub SN74			X	1			Sub SA90		X	Unused Sub		Unused Sub		Sub DS81	Unused Sub	Unused Sub													
34	1	Unused Sub	Unused Sub			X	Sub ED65 1		Unused Sub			Unused Sub	1	Unused Sub																	
35	X	1 x		Unused Sub	1		Sub NDJ78	Unused Sub		X	Sub SS45		Unused Sub			Unused Sub	Unused Sub														
36	X	Sub JL68	Sub GB86	X		Sub JM62		1	Unused Sub	1 x		Unused Sub	X	Unused Sub																	
37	1		Sub SA80	Sub SN54		1			1 x	Unused Sub	Unused Sub	X		Unused Sub	Sub AJ84	X									Unused Sub			Debut AJ90			
38	Sub DS90	1			X	Sub SA89			X	Unused Sub	Unused Sub	X		Unused Sub	Unused Sub	AJ84													Unused Sub		
39	Sub DS82				X	Unused Sub	X		X		Unused Sub	Sub MB78 1	Sub SN88	Unused Sub	X														Unused Sub		
40			Sub GB58	1	Sub SN69 1	Unused Sub	X		Sub DS76		Unused Sub	1		Unused Sub															Sub SA80 1		
41	Unused Sub		Sub YT86		Sub MB79 1	1 x		1	1 x	Unused Sub	Unused Sub		1																Sub AJ71		
42		Unused Sub	X	Sub SN84	Unused Sub	Sub DP62	1		1	Unused Sub	X	Unused Sub		X	Unused Sub	PZ19													X		
43		Sub VK12	X		X				Sub ED71	X	Unused Sub		Unused Sub		Sub GB59														Unused Sub		
44		Unused Sub	X	Unused Sub	X	Sub DS87		X	Sub NDJ84	Unused Sub	Sub GB38		Unused Sub																Unused Sub		
45		Sub AJ46		Unused Sub	X	Sub DP55	1	Unused Sub		2			Unused Sub	Sub DS66															X	Unused Sub	
46	Unused Sub	X		Unused Sub	X	Sub DS76		X	Sub MB45		Sub NDJ66		Unused Sub	1																	
47	Unused Sub	Unused Sub	1	Sub PZ84		X	Sub DS72	Unused Sub			Sub GB74		Unused Sub																		
48	X	1		X	X		2	Unused Sub	Sub MR46	Unused Sub	Unused Sub		Sub DS58																Sub JM81		
49	Unused Sub	Sub SN79	Unused Sub	X		Unused Sub	■		X		Sub SA83	Unused Sub	X																Sub YT17		
50		Unused Sub			Unused Sub 1 x	Sub SA74		Sub CT63				2 x	Sub DS81	1 x	Unused Sub														Unused Sub		
51	Sub CT82		Unused Sub	Sub SN63	Unused Sub			Unused Sub		Sub DS76 1			2	3 x	X	Unused Sub															
52			Unused Sub	Sub DS59	Unused Sub	X		Unused Sub		Sub CT75			1	X	Unused Sub	1 x		Sub SN86													
53	Sub DS82		1	Unused Sub	Sub CT68		X	Sub SN93		Unused Sub	Unused Sub			X	Unused Sub																
54	Sub DS86		Unused Sub	Sub SN62	2		X		Sub CT70		Unused Sub			X	Unused Sub																
55	Unused Sub		Unused Sub	Sub YT44	X				Sub GB69 1	Sub CT75	X			1	Unused Sub																

GARDEN OF EDIN

Draped in the colours of Bosnia and Herzegovina, and sporting a City fan's jester hat, goal-hero Edin Dzeko, proudly shows off his Premier League winners' medal as the on-pitch party continues

SILVER WHERE?

If you look closely you can see it...
Captain Vincent Kompany proudly walks
around the Etihad Stadium with the Premier
League trophy raised above his head for
the fans to soak up and watch it glisten

"

This is a great day for City and most of all for the supporters. It has been 44 years since this club last had their hands on the title and everyone at City knows that is too long. We did it the hard way but I am told that is the City way. The supporters have never lost faith or patience – even in the last five minutes today – and we are so pleased that this season we have delivered some history for them

"

– ROBERTO MANCINI, MAY 13, 2012